Jesus Hopped the 'A' Train

Stephen Adly Guirgis is a proud, long-time member of LAByrinth Theater Company in New York. *Jesus Hopped the 'A' Train* has been performed to great acclaim Off-Broadway and at the Edinburgh Festival 2001 where it received a Fringe First award. *Jesus Hopped the 'A' Train* runs in 2002 in the United States at Chicago's Steppenwolf Theater, with productions scheduled around America and in Finland. His previous play *In Arabia We'd All Be Kings*, originally produced by LAByrinth and voted one of the Ten Best Plays of 1999 by *Time Out* New York, will receive its British premiere as part of the 2003 first season of the re-opened Hampstead Theatre, London and will be published by Methuen. His new play *Our Lady of 121st Street* premieres at New York City's LAByrinth in summer 2002.

Published by Methuen 2002

3 5 7 9 10 8 6 4 2

First published in 2002 by
Methuen Publishing Limited
215 Vauxhall Bridge Road,
London SW1V 1EJ

Methuen Publishing Limited Reg. No. 3543167

The author has asserted his moral rights.

A CIP catalogue record is available from the British Library

ISBN 0 413 77213 6

Typeset by SX Composing DTP, Rayleigh, Essex
Printed and bound in Great Britain by
Cox & Wyman Ltd, Reading, Berkshire

 The publishers are grateful to the Donmar Warehouse
for providing the cover image.

Jesus Hopped the 'A' Train

Stephen Adly Guirgis

Methuen Drama

Jesus Hopped the 'A' Train was originally produced by
LAByrinth Theater Company in New York and
subsequently produced Off-Broadway in New York by Ron
Kastner, Roy Gabay and John Gould Rubin. It was also
performed at the Edinburgh Fringe Festival and received its
London premiere at the Donmar Warehouse on 11 March
2002. The cast was in order of speaking as follows:

Angel Cruz	John Ortiz
Lucius Jenkins	Ron Cephas Jones
Valdez	David Zayas
Mary Jane Hanrahan	Elizabeth Canavan
D'Amico	Salvatore Inzerillo

Director Philip Seymour Hoffman
Designer Narelle Sissons
Costume Designer Mimi O'Donnell
Lighting Designer Sarah Sidman
Sound Designer Eric DeArmon

The action of the play takes place in New York City's
criminal justice system, largely in the yard of a special
twenty-three-hour lockdown wing of protective custody on
Riker's Island.

This play is dedicated to David Hoghe (1963–2000).

Act One

Scene One

Manhattan correctional center, 'the Tombs' darkness. Late night.
Angel Cruz, *alone, tries to pray.*

Angel 'Our Father, who art in heaven, Howard be Thy name. Howard? How art? how? –How-now? . . . Fuck!!!! Motherfuckah . . . Fuckin' . . . 'Our Father, who aren't in heaven' . . . who aren't?! Fuck! who – 'Our Father who art– (who art!!), Our Father who art in Heaven, how- how-, how-, howl-ed, how-led, howling, howl, howl, Thurston Howell, fuckin', fuckin', SHIT!!!

Inmate 1 Shut the fuck up!!!

Angel 'Our Father who art in heaven, how-, how-, how-, fuck, how-, how-, how-, goddamn it, how-, how-, how –

Inmate 1 'How, how, how' my ass, mothahfuckah! Niggahs tryin to sleep up in this mothahfuckah!

Angel 'Our Father' –

Inmate 1 Shut the fuck up!

Angel 'Our Father' –

Inmate 1 Shut the fuck up!

Angel 'Our Father' –

Inmate 1 Shut the fuckety fuck up!

Angel You shut the fuckety fuck up!

Inmate 1 You shut the fuckety fuck up!

Inmate 2 Both a y'all, shut the fuck up!

Inmate 1 (*to* **Inmate 2**) Who you tellin', 'shut the fuck up'? You shut the fuck up!

Angel 'Our Father' –

Inmate 2 (*to* **Inmate 2**)   I know you ain't tellin' me shut the fuck up!

Angel   'Our Father' –

Inmate (*to* **Inmate 2**)   I'm tellin you and that prayin' niggah, shut the fuck up!

Angel   'Our father who art in heaven' –

Inmate 2 (*to* **Inmate 1**)   Don't tell me shut the fuck up!

Inmate (*to* **Inmate 2**)   Shut the fuck up!

Inmate 2 (*to* **Inmate 2**)   You shut the fuck-up!

Inmate 3   All y'all niggahs best shut the fuck up!!

Angel   'Our father who art in heaven'

Inmates 1, 2, and **3**   Shut the fuck up!!!!

Angel   'Hal- Hal-Hallowed! Hallowed be thy name!'

Inmate 3   We'll see you up at Riker's, mothahfuckah!

Angel   'Thy Kings will come' –

Inmate 1   Shut the fuck up!

Angel   You shut the fuck up!

Inmate 1   Shut the fuckety fuck up!

Inmate 2   We gonna kill you, Cruz!

Angel   I'll kill all a y'all!! I'll kill all a y'all little bitches!

A **Guard** *enters, club in hand.*

Guard   Hey! What's goin' on in here?!

Inmate 1   Crip out.

Inmate 2   Crip out.

Angel   Whatch'all tryin' ta say? You crips? Fuck the crips!

Guard   Hey!

Angel   Fuck crips!!

Guard   Cruz, since this is your first night with us –

Angel   – 'Our Father, who art in heaven' –

Guard   Hey!

Angel   'Our Father, who – who – who' –

Guard   Cruz!

Angel   Our Father –

Guard   Shut the fuck up!

Angel   Fuck you!

Guard   What?!

Angel   Our Father –

Guard   Fuck me?!

Angel   'Our father – who art in heaven' –

Guard   Fuck me?!

Angel   'Hallowed be thy name, hallowed be thy name' –

The **Guard** *enters* **Angel***'s cell.*

Guard   Did you just say: 'Fuck me'?!

Lights crossfade.

Valdez   I know an ex-con who did seven years for murdering a nice hot-dog vendor. He slept soundly every night, undisturbed by his conscience. He now lives at Gun Hill Road in the Bronx, so, beware if you happen to be around that area. He has no regard for human life, including his own. I would like to take his late-model Sports Utility Vehicle and drive it through his front door, accelerate past his bathroom, and come to a violent, crashing halt right on top of his head, but . . . the law prohibits me. Instead, I simply wish that he dies soon and painfully . . . Whenevah I see him, I say: 'I wish you die soon and painfully' . . . Before I became a corrections officer, I worked for the Department of Sanitation hauling garbage. It used to amaze me, the valuable items people would cavalierly discard. It angered me. Couches, alarm-clock radios, family photos. I often wanted to go to people's apartments and throttle them. One time I saw a guy throw out a very nice color television set. I asked him if it still worked. He said, 'Yes.' I asked him why he didn't just give it away instead of trashing it. He smirked at me. I slapped him. People think everything is replaceable. Everything is not replaceable. People believe they go through life accumulating things. That is incorrect. People go through life discarding things, tangible and intangible, replaceable and priceless. What people do not understand is that once they have discarded an irreplaceable item, it is lost for ever . . .

Blackout.

Scene Two

Manhattan correctional center, legal consultations room. **Mary Jane** *and* **Angel** *(beaten up) midstream.*

Angel – What I want is a fuckin' lawyer! Is it possible, in this nightmare – I mean, what the fuck is this?! – Even on TV they get a lawyer –

Mary Jane I am a lawyer, I'm your lawyer –

Angel I wanna real lawyer!

Mary Jane I am a real lawyer, and you are my real client –

Angel Fuck that!

Mary Jane You wanna see the paperwork?

Angel   Fuck the paperwork! Why didn't you check the paperwork before you came in here talkin all kinda shit when you didn't even know who you was speakin' to?

Mary Jane   Look, I am sorry for the mix-up, I –

Angel   The 'mix-up'? Is that what just happened before? We had a little 'mix-up'?!

Mary Jane   I said –

Angel   – Do you always have these little 'mix-ups'? Or do you just never know who anybody is?

Mary Jane   I'm sorry!

Angel   I ain't Hector Villanueva!

Mary Jane   I know that –

Angel   Hector Villanueva: No Aqui!

Mary Jane   OK, What I need from you –

Angel   Need?! You gonna sit there and talk to me about what you need? I'm incarcerated, lady! Why can't we talk about what I fuckin' need?!

Mary Jane   What do you need?

Angel   I need a damn lawyer!

Mary Jane   Which is why I'm here –

Angel   This is bullshit! This is racism is what it is, racism!! If I was white, I'd have motherfuckin' Perry Mason sittin here wit the little glasses and the beard talkin fuckin' strategy. Instead they give me some bumblin'-ass Wilma Flintstone don't even know who I am!!

Mary Jane   You're Angel Cruz, you're thirty years old, you live with your mom on Tiemen Place, West Harlem. You have one felony prior, a robbery, you were sixteen. You work as a bike messenger. You had a year of college, you played soccer –

Angel   I never played soccer!!

Mary Jane   You're charged with attempted murder, I know that.

Angel   Attempted murder?! –

Mary Jane   That surprises you? –

Angel   – Ya see, Bitch? Dass exactly what I'm talkin 'bout! All I did –

Mary Jane   – Stop!

Angel   All I did was shoot him in the ass, what the fuck is 'attempted murder' about that, huh?! . . . Stupid ass! . . .

Mary Jane *rises, begins collecting her things.*

Angel   What are you doing?

Mary Jane   I'm leaving.

Angel   Why, 'cuz I called you a bitch?

Mary Jane   No, because you just confessed to me.

Angel   Confessed? Confessed what?

Mary Jane   You just admitted to me that you did the shooting.

Angel   No I didn't!

Mary Jane   You just said: 'All I did was shoot him in the ass.'

Angel   So?

Mary Jane   So now you get your wish: I can't adequately defend you now, so you'll get another lawyer.

Angel   What if I don't want another lawyer?

Mary Jane   You just got through haranguing me –

Angel   'Haranguing'?

Mary Jane   Haranguing: it means –

Angel   I know what the fuck it means. Whaddya think?
I'm a Puerto Rican, therefore I'm a motherfuckah who can't
know shit?

Mary Jane   Yeah, that's exactly what I was thinking –

Angel   I know a lot a fuckin' shit!

Mary Jane   Well then, know this: When the next lawyer
walks in here, tomorrow, or the day after, try not to confess
to him –

Angel   Tomorrow?! –

Mary Jane   Because when you confess to your lawyer,
Angel, it means we can't put you on the witness stand –

Angel   – Hold up –

Mary Jane   Because if we did put you on the witness
stand, we would be suborning perjury and I'm sure, of
course, that you know what 'suborning' means, but on the
off chance you might've missed that vocabulary word during
your high school years at Power Memorial, let me refresh
you: it means if you're lying up there, we can't know about
it –

Angel   OK –

Mary Jane   – And if we do know about it, we're obligated
to inform the court –

Angel   So –

Mary Jane   – And if we don't inform the court and
someone finds out about it, then we get in a lot of trouble!

Angel   If you had toal me this shit before –

Mary Jane   And another thing: if a public defender
confuses you with someone else, it might be because they
have dozens of other cases and they made an honest
mistake! This is the criminal justice system you're in now.
Mix-ups happen here! –

Angel   – So whatchu gonna do about it?!

Mary Jane   What am I gonna do? –

Angel   – 'Cuz I ain't got 'till tomorrow –

Mary Jane   Lemme give you a little tip: The trick, Angel, is not to have a lawyer who makes no mistakes, but to get the lawyer who a) makes the least mistakes, and b) is either green enough or masochistic enough to actually give a shit about their clients.

Angel   So which one are you?

Mary Jane   I'm neither.

Mary Jane *exits.*

Blackout.

Scene Three

The yard, protective custody, Rikers Island. **Lucius Jenkins***, an older inmate, is in an outdoor cage burning through the end of a vigorous workout.* **D'Amico** *rises from his seated post.*

D'Amico   Still workin out, huh, Lou?

Lucius   Feelin good, Brother Charlie, in fine feather! How'm I looking?

D'Amico   Lookin' good, Lou.

Lucius   Ever tell you I was a champion swimmer and springboard diver in high school?

D'Amico   Were ya?

Lucius   Back in the day, brother, back in the day. Olympic caliber . . . Got a cigarette for me, brother?

D'Amico   Sure thing, Lou.

Lucius   Gimme another one for behind my ear . . . The Lord loves ya, Charlie.

D'Amico   Thanks, Lou . . .

Lucius   Dig that sun, Charlie.

D'Amico   Yup.

Lucius   Sun shines on me, sun shines on you.

D'Amico   Yup.

Lucius   It ain't sunnier over there by you, is it?

D'Amico   Nope.

Lucius   You got dat right. Praise Be!

D'Amico   Could I ax you sumptin', Lou?

Lucius   You ain't messin' up again, are ya, brother?

D'Amico   Nah, it's just, I heard you turned down an interview, some kinda life story on *Court TV*?

Lucius   Television's the number-one narcotic we got going on up here in America! Keeps a man idle and stupid. Might as well pump heroin into the airstream. Same difference . . . TV!! Ha!! . . . *Who Wants To Be A Millionaire?*! *Who Wants To Kiss My Narrow Black Ass?*, I'd say that's a lot more like it. And that's pretty much what I told them TV folks.

D'Amico   Yeah, well, my wife's a little disappointed, thought I might get a little screen time, somethin' to tell the relatives.

Lucius   You did thank her for that fine shepherd's pie she made me?

D'Amico   I did.

Lucius   Tell her sorry 'bout the interview, Lucius don't do no TV . . . Unless, of course, they bring that Connie Chung up in here, kinda like her, Lord forgive me . . . Say, Charlie, about them Oreo cookies –

D'Amico   You didn't see them? I left them in your cell.

Lucius   Yeah, brother, I found them all right, and God
bless ya for it, but the thing is, they got these other kinda
Oreos –

D'Amico   What kind?

Lucius   They got this kind that's dipped in fudge, that's
the kind I was talkin' about the other day.

D'Amico   I'm sorry, Lucius, I didn't realize –

Lucius   Quite all right, brother, quite all right. Now
here's the thing: these fudge-dipped little concoctions, they
come in chocolate fudge and Vanilla fudge –

D'Amico   Chocolate and vanilla.

Lucius   I like the vanilla fudge, that it is to say, The
Vanilla Fudge, that's where my preference lies, if ya get my
meaning.

D'Amico   Not a problem, Lou. I'll juss tell my wife; she'll
be happy to do it.

Lucius   Your wife's a fine woman, Charlie.

D'Amico   I know.

Lucius   But then again, why wouldn't she be, since you
such a fine gentleman yourself.

D'Amico   Thanks, Lou.

Lucius   And I mean that sincerely.

D'Amico   Me too.

Lucius   Praise be . . . So whatchu think, Charlie? I'm a
beat extradition?

D'Amico   Sure, Lou. Why not?

Lucius   Juss like you gonna beat what needs beatin',
right?

D'Amico   Damn straight, Lou.

Lucius 'We all gonna beat . . . what needs to be beat . . . so we can snatch vict'ry . . . from the jaws of defeat!'

D'Amico   I like that. Who said it?

Lucius   Your mother.

D'Amico   What?

Lucius   I said it, Charlie, juss made it up now.

D'Amico   Oh.

Lucius   'Gotta stay wit me, baby' –

D'Amico   – I'm here Lou –

Lucius   Sharp minds think alike.

D'Amico   'Sharp minds, sharp products.'

Lucius   What's that?

D'Amico   You never heard that before?

Lucius   Nah, man.

D'Amico   Really?

Lucius   Who in the world said that?

D'Amico   Your grandma.

Lucius   My . . . ? Oh now, Charlie, you are a wicked, sinful man –

D'Amico   That I am.

Lucius   If my ol' granny were here now she'd flatten you like a thin-crust pizza, you could believe that!

Valdez *enters, eating from a box of Oreos.*

Valdez   Officer D'Amico! Superintendent Callahan wants to see you in his office.

D'Amico   What for?

Valdez   I'm afraid I am not privy to that information.

D'Amico   All right, let me just secure the prisoner back to his cell –

Valdez   He wants to see you now.

D'Amico   Like, right this second?

Valdez   Pronto. His words, not mine.

D'Amico   OK. Uh –

Valdez   I'll secure the prisoner.

D'Amico   Do you know how to do it?

Valdez   Do I know how to do it? Yes, I think I do.

D'Amico   Lucius doesn't give us much of a problem –

Valdez   I'm sure he won't.

D'Amico   OK then.

D'Amico *exits.*

Lucius   Didn't catch your name.

Valdez   Valdez.

Lucius   Valdez?

Valdez   Correct.

Lucius   Fine day today, huh, Valdez?

Valdez   Splendid. Step away from the cage.

Lucius   You don't mind if I linger a little, do ya, brother?

Valdez   Linger?

Lucius   Enjoy a few more minutes of this Heaven-Sent Autumn Breeze, just, you know, till Charlie gets back?

Valdez   'Charlie' will not be returning.

Lucius   Gone for the day?

Valdez   Gone. Step away from the cage.

Lucius   You a church-goin' man?

Valdez   I worship the devil. Away from the cage.

Lucius   Thing is, I'd really prefer –

Valdez   You'd prefer?

Lucius   Just a couple more minutes, put my thoughts in order –

Valdez   When you're back in your cell, you're gonna have all the time you need for reflection. Last time: step away.

Lucius   Yeah, I see your point, big man, I do indeed. Thing is, up here in PC, up here, it's a little different than downstairs. We gotta different kinda vibe going on –

Valdez   'Vibe'?

Lucius   Yeah, brother man, it's a different kinda feel –

Valdez   'Feel'?

Lucius   Works out nicely for everybody.

Valdez   Oh . . . Well, let me, if I may, tell you now about my vibe, my feel . . . My 'vibe' is: step away from that cage before I come in there and club you to death.

Lucius   'Nuff said, brother, 'nuff said.

Lucius *assumes the position.* **Valdez** *enters the cage, cuffs him.*

Valdez   Nah, nah, I juss told you about my vibe. Now lemme tell you about my 'feel' . . . Now stand up. Thank you. My 'feel' is this:

He spits in **Lucius***'s face.*

Thass my feel. It's a 'different kinda feel', I know, but – it's my feel. And if you gotta problem with my feel, then you are gonna get a taste of my vibe. Are we clear on the 'Vibe and Feel' thing now?

Lucius   Affirmative.

Valdez   This is not Jellystone Park. I am not the Park
Ranger. There will be no more Oreo cookies in your Picnic
Basket. There will be no more Picnic . . . Got that,
Superstar? . . . I do not like Infractions. There will be no
more Infractions. At this moment, I give you zero respect
because that's where your balance stands. Zero . . . That's
why I can spit in your face. That's why I am currently eye-
balling you in an aggressive manner, eating your cookies . . .
That's why I can tell you that in my mind, you're a
worthless psychopathic piece of shit, a scrawny old HIV
faggot, a skin-poppin' ugly, gangly bag of bones – an
eyesore . . . 'Black Plague': that's what they call you, right?
'Cuz you Black and you killed a lot a motherfuckahs'? . . . I
heard you give out autographs –

Lucius   Prayer cards –

Valdez   You think you some kind a superstar, Mr
Superstar?

Lucius   I'm a God-fearing man.

Valdez   Don't be a God-fearing man, be a Valdez-fearing
man . . . I heard they wanna put you on TV, lemme tell you
something about that: I enjoy TV. I would go so far as to
say that I love TV. I gotta big-screen TV in my den, I watch
it often with Popcorn and Pepsi. If I ever see you on the TV
being a Superstar, it will upset me. And if that happens, I'm
gonna come back to work here the next day and I'm gonna
do a little 'Vibe and Feel' on your ass. Understood?

Lucius   Yeah, man.

Valdez   Say: 'Affirmative.' Say it!

Lucius   Affirmative.

Valdez   Goddamn right, Superstar. If you do not fuck
with me, Mr Superstar, I can guarantee you a garden-
variety miserable existence. But if you do decide to fuck with
me – ever – I will show you a world where mere misery is

like toasting marshmallows 'round the campfire in your long johns. You get me, Superstar?

Lucius   The Lord will provide.

Valdez   Excuse me?

Lucius   I mean, 'Affirmative.'

Valdez   I don't give a fuck what you mean. When they extradite your ass to Florida, you can resume your shenanigans. Until then, Believe This: If you ever try to wave a Bible in my face, I'll shove it right through your teeth. And don't you ever ask me for no cigarette, 'cuz I don't smoke. Move it out!

Scene Four

Mary Jane *speaks*.

Mary Jane   Angel Cruz had said: 'All I did was shoot him in the ass' . . . There was something so juvenile about that, obviously . . . but, for me, although I wasn't aware of it at the time, there was also something familiar and . . . nostalgic . . . When I was fifteen, there had been this Father/ Daughter Dance at the Elite Private Girls' School in Manhattan that I went to as a charity case-slash-financial aid recipient. My mother had, wisely, arranged for her brother, Uncle Mikey, to take me to the Dance, but at the last minute, my father decided that him not escorting me himself might be one of those things that might scar me in later life – so – me and my father left our two-family house in Sunnyside that evening; me in a dress my parents couldn't afford, and my dad in his Irish All Purpose Navy Blue Suit with a pair of black socks we had convinced him to borrow from the neighbors . . . When we got inside the ballroom, I took a quick look around and became instantly embarrassed to the point of humiliation by the fact that my dad was the only father on the Upper East Side that night whose suit pants didn't have cuffs. But within an hour,

everyone was calling him 'Danny', even The Headmistress,
who hadn't called me anything but 'Miss Hanrahan' in
three years. And he was dancing, and chatting; And he had
even stuck by the agreed-upon two-beer rule, or so I
thought . . . At some point in the evening, one of the other
fathers made an off-hand comment that my father took
exception to; a heated discussion ensued, and my father
ended up stabbing the guy with a dessert fork, breaking the
skin . . . What the guy had said was unimportant; actually,
what he said was, he was reminiscing about where he had
grown up as a kid and he remarked that: 'It used to be a
good neighborhood, you know, white, now, forget it, I went
back there last month, it's half white, the rest: blacks and
Italians.' My mom's Italian. EMS was called, and the
dance? – Well, let's just say the stabbing concluded the
dancing portion of the evening . . . My father's justification
for the assault, after explaining how he didn't immediately
attack him, and how he had given the 'rich jerk' ample
opportunity to apologize, and how he won't tolerate a bigot
no matter where he is, and: 'What if your mom or "Rasheed
from the Deli" had been there?', and how he still doesn't
understand why I need to go to that stuck-up school
anyway. In the end, what he finally said was: 'It was just a
fork' . . . And he said it, I've now come to realize, with just
that same look of incredulousness on his face that Angel
Cruz had on his . . . as if the whole world was crazy and he
was the only sane one . . . I hated my dad for the whole
mortifying incident, but the dysfunctional side of me was
proud of him – actually, I'm still kind of proud of him – and
I'm not convinced that there's something wrong with me for
feeling that. I had no idea why Angel Cruz had 'just shot
him in the ass' but I felt something – something – and I
needed to know what it was. And even though I was no
longer obligated to him as his counsel, and despite the fact
that the rational side of my brain was very much convinced
that he had, in fact, attempted to murder Reverend Kim,
and, yes, of course, even if he hadn't literally attempted
murder, you still can't run around shooting people just like

you can't go around stabbing people with dessert forks, I know all that, but, I gotta admit, that somewhere inside of me, and I don't know if it's the good side, or the side that I saw a therapist twice a week and went to ACOA meetings for, but somewhere inside of me is a place that believes that sometimes you can do those things, or at least, somebody can, or, should, and that one man's neurotic is another man's hero, and who, ultimately, can say which one's which with any real certainty at all? . . .

Scene Five

The yard. Protective custody, Rikers Island. **Lucius Jenkins** *is in his outdoor cage jogging furiously in place.*

Lucius   Lord, I believe, aid thou my disbelief! Lord, I believe, aid thou my disbelief! Devil, get thee gone, Devil, go away! Usurp the Serpent, Lord, he crawlin up my leg! Irrigate the Bile, Lord, ketchin in my neck! Take away the vengeance, Lord, swirlin in my vein! Lobotomize the evil, Lord, slinkin in my brain! . . . Can't go back, Can't go back Can't go back, Can't go back! . . . Watch me kick my knees up ta Heaven: . . . Through the Grace, I jog in place, where once was sloth, now I'm cookin broth! Cookin' broth, Jesus; Check the recipe! Old Testament Backwards!: 'Malachi, Zechariah, Haggai, Zephaniah, Habakkuk, Nahum, Micah, Jonah, Obadiah, Amos, Joel, Hosea, Daniel, Ezekiel, Lamentations, Jeremiah, Isiah, Song a Songs, Ecclesiastes, Proverbs, Psalms, Job, Esther, Nehemiah, Ezra, Chronicles 2, Chronicles 1, Kings 2, Kings 1, Samuel 2, Samuel 1, Ruth, Judges, Joshua, Deuteronomy, Numbers, Leviticus, Exodus, and Genesis, mothahfuckah, pardon my French!! . . . Make me a Mustard Seed, Jesus! Hold the damn Mayo, gimme the Mustard!! Ain't talkin 'bout Ketchup, I wants the Mustard! Don't relish the relish, don't need ta embellish, ain't tryin' ta get it on – Juss pass the Grey Poupon! . . . You like that one, Jesus? Gonna drop and give ya twenty, Baby! Watch me now . . . one, two three four, cuz I love you,

Lord, I'll do some more' (ya watchin?) 'eight nine ten
eleven, endure the pain, get ta heaven' (observe the rigid
form) 'fifteen sixteen seventeen eighteen, get me saved
before my date!' . . . Up and Adam, Adam and Eve . . .
Miles to go, Miles to go! 'The Harvest is plentiful, but the
workers are few!!' 'Harvest: Plentiful, Workers:Few! I'll work
hard, I'll produce a fine Harvest! . . . Gimme sumpthin' ta
work with, and we'll transform misery inta ministry, make a
prison a palace . . . Lord, make me an instrument of thy
peace.' Thy will be done! Deliver me from evil, Lord, Thy
will be done! Deliver me from me, Lord, deliver me from
me!

Valdez   Time!

Lucius   . . . I'll sprint for ya, faster, I'll sprint to Valhalla
and back, faster,

Valdez   Times Up!!

Lucius (*to* **Valdez**)   No it ain't! Sprint to Golgotha two
times, faster,

Valdez   Away from the cage, Jenkins!

Lucius   To Florida or the Promised Land, faster,

Valdez   Cease now!!

Lucius (*to* **Valdez**)   Time ain't up, check your Timex!
Ridin' with ya –

Valdez   You want a fuckin' war?!

Lucius *stops, assumes the position.* **Valdez** *enters.*

Valdez   I could dismantle that camera, assault you into a
coma, and suffer no penalty! In fact, I would 'prolly be
applauded . . . This little charade you're playin', this
communication with God: It's a farce.

Lucius   Well, now –

Valdez   Sheer folly.

Lucius   You believe in God, Valdez?

Valdez   I believe you are about one more syllable out
your mouth from death, mothahfuckah.

Lucius   I –

Valdez   No more God out here in the yard.

Lucius   What?!

Valdez   Do you need me to correct your hearing
problem?

Lucius   – Do you know who I am?!

Valdez   Do you?

Lucius   I got rights! It's in the Constitution!!

Valdez   What, you didn't hear of the latest judicial ruling?
The Supreme Court ruled in the case of 'Valdez versus The
Skinny Black Faggot', that the separation of Church and
State can only be superceded upon the separation of the
Skinny Black Faggot's limbs from his withered torso . . . In
other words, I am the Constitution. And you, you're a
Skinny Black Faggot . . . Questions? Comments? (*Looking up.*)
'God? Do You beg to differ?!' . . . (*To* **Lucius**.) Whoa! . . .
Wait a second, Mr Superduperstar: do I detect a droplet of
rage somewhere behind those con-man's eyes? . . . Silence? .
. . I like that. Thass promising . . . Some people call this
place the VIP lounge, that is inaccurate. You are here not
because you are a VIP, you are here because the rest of the
livestock downstairs wishes to cannibalize you. You are
livestock in storage and I am a Cowboy currently in charge
of just one Cow. Check your ass when you get back to your
cell. It says: 'Valdez, property of' . . . God hates you.

Blackout.

Scene Six

Manhattan correctional center, legal consultations room. **Angel** *alone, more beaten up.* **Mary Jane** *enters, tentatively.*

Mary Jane Hello, Angel –

Angel What are you doing here?

Mary Jane Came to check in on you.

Angel 'Check in on me'?

Mary Jane You don't look so good.

Angel The fuck you care?!

Mary Jane Angel –

Angel – Yo, I gotta visitor coming, so –

Mary Jane I didn't see anyone else's name in the log-book –

Angel Logbook?

Mary Jane When I signed in –

Angel They prolly ain't here yet –

Mary Jane Do you know who's coming?

Angel Not exactly. Somebody.

Mary Jane Regular visiting hours are, uh, over.

Angel Over?

Mary Jane . . . Yeah.

Angel . . . Oh.

Pause.

Mary Jane . . . Angel, I'm sorry about yesterday.

Angel What?

Mary Jane I said –

Angel   What time did visiting hours end?

Mary Jane   About a half-hour ago.

Angel   Was there people down there when you came in?

Mary Jane   Yeah.

Angel   So people could be down there, but maybe they don't get in?

Mary Jane   It happens a lot.

Angel   Did you, was there any white guys down there?

Mary Jane   Umm.

Angel   Like a guy my age with, like, black hair, curly, kinda look like me but white? Maybe he was wit' some Chinese-lookin' people, Korean?

Mary Jane   I don't think I saw anyone who looked like that, but –

Angel   No big deal.

Pause.

Mary Jane   I could check downstairs –

Angel   – Yo, Is there sumpthin' that you want?!

Pause.

Mary Jane   I, uh, I brought some food –

Angel   Food?

Mary Jane   I got some chicken, potato pancakes, cole-slaw, I also got some Ring Dings in here someplace and some donuts –

Angel   You didn't bring no deviled eggs?

Mary Jane   Deviled eggs?

Angel   Some deviled eggs and a little blanket, we could have a fuckin' picnic –

Mary Jane   Angel –

Angel   And we could invite some nice guests! Who you wanna invite?

Mary Jane   I'm just –

Angel   Tell you what: I'll invite my lawyer, and you could invite fuckin 'Hector Villanueva', and we'll party, cuz, thass what this is, right? A fuckin party? Let's, let's go get some 'opera music' and some Popsicle sticks and go see the fuckin' Shakespeare in the Park –

Mary Jane   – I could leave if you want.

Angel   Who's stoppin you?!

Mary Jane   But then they'd just return you to your cell.

Angel   Return me to my? Did you juss fuckin' threaten me?

Mary Jane   Did you shoot Reverend Kim with the intention of killing him?

Angel   Are you makin fuckin' threats?

Mary Jane   You went there to kill him, didn't you?

Angel   You ain't my lawyer no more.

Mary Jane   I know that –

Angel   – I got another lawyer now, much better than you. Got a beard and everything.

Mary Jane   I know.

Angel   Little half glasses, whaddya call them, bifocals? Nice suit, smart. Langdon Brown!

Mary Jane   I know Langdon.

Angel   Dass Right! Man's even writin' a screenplay! You ever write a fuckin' screenplay?!

Mary Jane   I'm too busy practicing law to write screenplays.

Angel   Yeah, well, Langdon Brown, he don't need ta practice, he already got that shit down!!

Mary Jane   Yeah, well . . .

Angel   He toal' me all about you too! Toal' me I could sue you if I wanted, make a complaint. Dass why you brought me chicken, right?

Mary Jane   I brought you –

Angel   Cuz if you wanted to bribe me, you shoulda brought me steak!

Mary Jane   This –

Angel   Big ol' steak, with a pair a Nuun Chucks –

Mary Jane   I'm –

Angel   Chainsaw inside the baked potato – Where you goin'?!

Mary Jane   Like I said –

Angel   You're a fuckin bitch, you know that?!

Mary Jane   I wish you all the best –

Angel   I don't need your wishes or your 'sorrys' or your chickens or your anything! I don't need anything!

Mary Jane   Angel –

Angel   Get the fuck outta here! Go on! Get out!

Mary Jane   Did you shoot Reverend Kim with the intention of killing him?!

Angel   I shot Reverend Kim in the ass with the intent to bust a cap in his lyin', bullshittin' ass!

Mary Jane   I don't believe that for a second!

Angel   I doan' give a shit what you believe! –

Mary Jane – What really happened? Were you ready to do it, but then you got scared and aimed low, is that it?

Angel Aimed low? I aimed for his damn ass and hit it. Mothahfuckah got an ass like a water buffalo, it ain't hard to locate!

Mary Jane But you wanted to kill him –

Angel I wanted to shoot him in the fuckin' ass, lady! How many times I gotta say it?

Mary Jane Why?

Angel It was something I could do, ah-aight?! These mothahfuckahs, like Reverend Kim, they run around, talkin' shit, talkin' 'God', and they steal people! Steal mothahfuckahs right out from your face. And what can you do about it? Nothin'! You go to The Law, you know what the law do? The law do fuckin' nothin', that's what the law do! You try to go to a outside agency, make a complaint: 'They stole my friend,' you know you talkin' to? You talkin' to the same mothahfuckahs who stole him in the first place! Juss like the, whaddyacallit, Scientologists and the Cult Awareness Network!

Mary Jane Scientologists? –

Angel Read the fuckin' paper, lady! Scientologists sued the Cult Awareness Network, bankrupted them, and took over the damn Cult Awareness Network! . . . Same office! Same phone number! But when you call the motherfuckahs up, you speaking to one of them! Now what kinda help you think they gonna give you?

Mary Jane So you went out, you got a gun –

Angel C'mon now! They didn't steal my friend yesterday! I didn't juss smoke a vial a crack, and bum rush the show 'guns a blazin''!

Mary Jane But you were high!

Angel   Look, I seen a seventy-five-year-old grandmother from Astoria get sent to penitentiary for trying to kidnap her grand-daughter from Reverend Kim's church! I kidnapped my friend Joey myself!

Mary Jane   When?

Angel   Two months ago! Two years in the makin'! Surveillance, kidnappers, fuckin' deprogrammer – you know what that is, right?

Mary Jane   I –

Angel   – Dass a expensive mothahfuckah: expensive and useless.

Mary Jane   It didn't work out.

Angel   Deprogrammer said Joey had an unusually strong faith, some bullshit – didn't stop him from cashin' the check!

Mary Jane   And you did this all yourself?

Angel   Nah, but it's amazin' how people act. One day they all, like: 'Yeah, bro, whatever ya need,' next day it's: 'Yo, fuck that niggah, B, got better things to do.' People, they forget.

Mary Jane   But not you.

Angel   Dass my friend! If someone's your friend, like, a real friend, how you supposed ta juss forget about him? You got any friends, lady?!

Mary Jane   Mary Jane –

Angel   You got any friends, 'Mary Jane'?! 'Cuz we got a friend, Eustace, he's doin' Life in Arizona, but we stopped hangin' wit him when we was like eleven! And we got this other friend, Crazy Legs, he died a cancer at twenty-two, and dass hard, but, at least he's dead! At least we could account for him, ya know? We'd go to the park, Grant's Tomb, smoke a joint, we'd save the last hit for Crazy Legs, put the roach to the side. Or playin' Chinese handball, you know, with the boxes?

Mary Jane   Ace, King, Queen –

Angel   When we'd play, don't matter how many people we got, the last box is for Lindsay Fernandez who can't play no more –

Mary Jane   Because?

Angel   Wheelchair, he ain't around, but again, at least I know why he's not around. But Joey? He juss gone. Bang: out! It'd be one thing if he was out for some good reason, like if he was an astronaut in space chasin' the cure for AIDS, but what he out for? He out for bullshit! He out 'cuz Reverend Kim sold him a straight-up lie–

Mary Jane   According to you –

Angel   According to me?! Do you know what Reverend Kim say?! He say he's the Son of God! I mean, how big does your fuckin' balls have to be to sit there with a straight face and claim some shit like that? Son a God?! Yo, even if there was a Son of God, which, I mean, get real– but –

Mary Jane   You don't believe in God?

Angel   Ah-aight, I'm a put it like this: if there was 'another' Son of God runnin' around here, juss pickin' up where his older brother left off, tryin' ta save our ass, he sure as shit ain't Reverend Kim! How many Sons of God you know drive a Lexus? Or got million-dollar stock portfolios? Or go skiing in Aspen? 'Cuz I'll tell you right now: if Jesus Christ existed, and I ain't sayin' he did, but if, by some miracle he actually did, The Mothahfuckah Didn't Ski!!

Mary Jane   Not in Israel he didn't –

Angel   Not in Israel, not nowhere! Swear ta God, I can't understan' why Joey don't see that! Dumb-ass mothahfuckah! It's so obvious, so clear, I mean, you wanna hear the fuckin', the 'know what I'm sayin'?– the, the irony?

The irony is this: me and Joey, we got, like, the telepathy: He always know what I'm thinkin' and vice versa the other way. I know what girl he like before he know it! he know what I'm gonna say, it ain't even come out my mouth yet! People think I'm crazy to have got involved in this shit the way I have, two years of my life and all that, maybe a lot more now, but, for real: if the situations was reversed, and it was me in that cult, no doubt in my mind Joey woulda done the same thing for me, only he prolly woulda did it better. He wouldn't a forgotten about me –

Mary Jane   – How about now?

Angel   'How 'bout now' what?!

Mary Jane   Where's your friend Joey now? You're in jail! Where's Joey?

Angel   It's 'cuz a –

Mary Jane   Because of what?!

Angel   He, he captured!

Mary Jane   He's not captured, you're captured! You been here, what? three days?!

Angel   Maybe he don't know I'm here –

Mary Jane   What? he doesn't read the papers?

Angel   I don't know what he reads –

Mary Jane   – Did it ever occur to you, Angel, that we, as individual people, are responsible for the individual choices that we make? And regardless of how close we may think we are to someone else, we have very little control over their choices, and absolutely zero responsibility for the consequences those choices bring on them?

Angel   Zero?

Mary Jane   That's right, zero!

Angel   Maybe for you –

Mary Jane   No! Not just for me, for everybody! If somebody joins some stupid cult, whether they're a good person or not, whether I love them or hate them, or think they're better than me, or think they've been manipulated, or abused, there's nothing I can do about it! Nothing! And it doesn't matter if that person is a total stranger or my sister; they aren't going to leave unless they want to, no matter what I think or feel!

Angel   Dass bullshit –

Mary Jane   My father was still smoking cigarettes while he was in an oxygen tent! I begged him to quit all my life, did it stop him from killing himself?

Angel   Maybe you shoulda tried harder! –

Mary Jane   – Harder than what? –

Angel   – Or maybe you didn't really give enough of a fuck to really try to help him!

Mary Jane   Should I have gone to the Chairman of Philip Morris and shot him in the ass?! Would that have helped him?!

Angel   . . . Maybe you should ax yourself that question!

Pause.

Mary Jane   That's ridiculous.

Angel   Is it?! My friend Joey should be doing what you're doing! He should be a public defender, or a drug counselor, helpin' the people, fuckin' whatever! But where is he? He's out! Gone! And why? Why is he not here? Why? Do you believe that Reverend Kim with his money and his power and his sports cars, do you believe that he's the actual Son of God?! That a man deported from his own country and convicted of tax evasion in this one could even speak for God, let alone be God? That a man who steals people, has them selling flowers on the street, gettin' rich off them, what the fuck? look me in my eye and tell me that a man like that

should be allowed to do what he's doing! With a fuckin'
government-approved tax-exempt status and a full police
escort?!

Mary Jane   Angel –

Angel   Where's my mother's full police escort when she
gets off the subway from work after midnight and has to
walk home alone? Where's Mother Teresa's Lexus? And
how 'bout you? You a public defender, and if you're any
good at lawyering at all, you could prolly make a lot more
money working someplace else, right? But you don't do
that, do you? So where's your mansion? Where's your
frappacino, swimming pool, mistress, Son a God fuckin'
wonderland, huh?! He stole my friend. I shot him in the ass.
Now I'm fucked in jail, and he's eating banana cream pie in
some plush hospital bed, lickin' his lips, reading the *Wall
Street Journal.* Juss like the chairman of Philip Morris! Your
pops, he six feet under, fuckin' maggot food now, Where's
the chairman? I'll tell you where the fuckin' chairman is!
Out there on the eighteenth green sippin' a Heineken,
wiping the crumbs from his shrimp salad sandwich off of his
cashmere sweater, and he's smiling, unaffected. Or am I just
being 'ridiculous'?!

Pause.

Mary Jane   Everything you're telling me, Angel, it's
sounds like a real good motive to wanna murder somebody.

Angel   My question to you was: is it ridiculous? . . . Guard!

Scene Seven

The yard, protective custody, a month later. **Mary Jane** *speaks as*
Lucius Jenkins *is led into his cage.* **Valdez** *exits.*

Mary Jane   Angel got to me. He got to me and I knew for
a fact I'd do a hell of a lot better for him then Langdon
Brown would. I might've been going through a tough time;

I had been struggling to care about anything I was doing in
a courtroom, but, unlike Langdon, at least I had the
capacity to care. And I did care. And it felt good to care. It
did. And I had to concede that what Angel, was saying was
not ridiculous. What was ridiculous was the fact that I
regularly earned acquittals for hardened career criminals:
crack dealers, arsonists, murderers even, people with jaw-
dropping rap sheets, and then, six months later, I'd be
asking bail for the same guy for the same offense or worse!
Angel wasn't a recidivist felon, he was a civilian. I believed I
could get Angel an acquittal without having to put him on
the stand. I believed that the jury, if led, wouldn't convict
Angel despite all the evidence . . . I could have plea-
bargained Angel's case; that would have been easy, routine
– most of those young district attorneys feared me because I
was that rare public defender who could ruin them by
taking an open-and-shut case to trial and win anyway cuz I
am – I was – a goddamn excellent attorney! I wouldn't plea
bargain Angel's case because: right after our second
meeting, he went back upstairs and was assaulted by two
other inmates– beaten and raped. I wouldn't plea-bargain
Angel's case because: three days later, when the Associated
Press reported that Reverend Kim had been rushed back to
surgery and that he had died on the operating table, Angel
was found unconscious in his cell the next morning with a
bedsheet tied around his neck. I wouldn't plea-bargain
Angel's case because: after Angel spent the next seventy-two
hours in a prison psych ward and before being transferred to
a special twenty-three-hour lockdown wing of protective
custody, I sat Angel down and informed him that the DA
had filed for first-degree felony murder and that the charge
carried a mandatory sentence of 'Life without the
Possibility'. And Angel looked at me, and said, 'Without the
possibility of what?'

Valdez *re-enters, leading* **Angel** *to his cage.*

Valdez   – 'But if you do decide to fuck with me – ever – I
will show you a world where mere misery is like toasting

marshmallows 'round the campfire in your long johns'. You
get me there, Droopy Dog? . . . Hey! . . . You like to pout?
Thass OK, you could pout . . . Don't pout too much,
though. I might start feelin' bad, and have to come in there
and . . . pet you . . . (*To* **Lucius**.) . . . Superstar?! . . . . .
Florida . . .

Valdez *retires to his post upstage center.*

Lucius   Hey, there, youngfella . . . I say, hey there,
brother . . . What's your name? . . . What's your name,
man? . . . Not up for conversatin'? . . . Dass OK, I
understand . . . Don't make much sense to stare at the
ground like that, though . . . You oughta be enjoyin' this sun
while you can feel it, brother . . . Don't come out but one
hour a day for us up here . . . One hour . . . I take my hour,
too. Don't matter if it's snowin', rainin', fire and brimstone,
nuclear attack, they gonna bring me out here! I'm a take my
one hour, you could bet on that! . . . I love me some sun . . .
Love it! . . . You know, they got a country over there in
Europe gets almost no sun whatsoever? It's true. That's a
bunch a pale Europeans drinkin coffee over there, ain't no
denyin' that. Feel bad for 'em. Takin' no sun's like drinkin'
no milk, depletes a man. Not a good prescription for mental
health, I'll tell ya that right now . . . Dass why you gotta take
your one hour no matter what. Some men, they stop takin
their hour, next thing ya know – . . . well . . . I take my
hour, and you should too! . . . Don't talk for a month, never
talk again, but take your damn hour, enjoy whatever type a
weather been provided . . . Especially sun . . . Yes, sir . . .
'Specially the sunshine. Didn't usta feel that way 'bout the
sunshine, back in the day . . . Betcha didn't know dat . . .
No, sir . . . No way . . . Could ya juss tell me your name? . . .
Ya do speak the King's English, doncha, son? I don't know
much Spanish 'cept: '*Yo quiero uno 8-ball de Ko-kai-Yeno*'!! Usta
say that all the time!

Valdez   You two ain't makin' love over there, are ya?

Lucius   Mothah – . . . See now, thass wrong! . . . Wrong!!!
Man tryin' ta vex me! . . . Man tryin' ta . . . Damn!!

Pause.

Angel   Angel.

Lucius   What's that?

Angel   . . . Angel.

Lucius   Angel?! . . . I like that name . . . Thass a fine
name. Say, Angel, would ya like a cigarette?

Angel   . . . Nah.

Lucius   Nah?

Angel   No thanks.

Lucius   You're smart ta say no. Learnin' the ropes . . .
But, see, me, I don't want nuthin' in return for this cigarette,
know what I'm sayin? I'm not lookin for a wifey. Don't close
my eyes and pretend you're my Aunt Mary . . . C'mon, son,
have a cigarette.

Angel   Nah . . .

Lucius   Now whaddya think? My dick's big enough to
reach into your cage over there, wrestle ya to the ground,
and insert itself up into ya? Hell, even Goliath wasn't hung
that strong . . . We in lockdown, kid . . . No contact never
. . . This is juss a friendly gesture, fact, it ain't even a friendly
gesture, it's what ya might call 'humanitarian aid'. Smoke
Lucky's?

Angel   . . . Nah.

Lucius   They'll bring ya luck . . . Tell ya what I'm gonna
do.

He looks toward **Valdez**.

 I'm a throw this here Lucky over to you with the matches.
After ya light that Lucky, I'd appreciate it if you'd send the

matches back my way. OK? . . . Here goes . . . There . . . Ya
got it?

Angel *looks toward* **Valdez**.

Angel   Nah . . . Here.

Angel *tosses cigarette and matches back to* **Lucius**.

Lucius   What'cha doin', youngblood? C'mon, baby, take
it easy . . . Easy . . . Dass a gift, me to you, ain't no thing. No
cause for alarm, no fire in the hole . . . Doan worry 'bout
that fool over there, he eatin' Cheese Doodles . . . C'mon,
. . . This is simple like arithmetic, brother . . . OK? . . .
Journey of a million miles, it commence itself on that first
step . . . Oh, c'mon . . . It's a cigarette, amigo, not a
engagement ring. OK? Check out my 'Hawthorne Wingo'
now.

He *arcs a perfectly soft hook shot with the cigarette/matches. They
land at* **Angel***'s feet.*

Heaven-sent, amigo, heaven-sent.

Pause.

Angel   . . . Thanks.

Lucius   Thank you, brother, thank you. Could ya send
over the matches, please? . . . Merci . . . Taste good?

Angel   Mmm.

Lucius   Like ya knew that it would! . . . Smokin's good for
ya, doan' let 'em tell ya otherwise: Let's a man stay humble.
'Cuz I figure, if a man successfully casts all his demons aside,
he might get cocky, start thinkin' he's invincible, perfect, or
somethin'. A man might start thinkin' he don't haveta
depend on, well . . . on higher entities. Surgeon General is
the general of what, anyway? He the general of the
surgeons!! Surgeons make money doin' them cancer
operations! Sound like there's a little reverse psychology
goin' on . . . Higher entities, they doan' bother wit the
double-talk, they come correct, jack . . . Yes they do . . .

Say, look at that seagull! . . . Nice, right? . . . I ain't bothered
to look at no wildlife in some time . . . Dass a nice flyin' bird
. . . Nice sun too . . . Hey, this is all right, ain't it? Two
gentlemen retirin' to the smokin' garden. No ice tea, but
thass OK. I'm Lucius Jenkins, ya heard of me, right?

Angel   The guard, he told me not ta –

Lucius   – Ya need ta forget about that guard, truss me.
That man is troubled, still searchin' for hisself . . . You need
ta remember one thing here, son: us – you and me, we here
cuz we have ta be. Got no choice in the matter. But that
man over there, he doan' haveta be here but he here
anyway! Now what that say 'bout him? This is New York
City, a man could work anywhere! Where he at? An doan'
tell me he raisin' a family, cuz, I'll wager every cigarette,
postage stamp, ramen noodle, I got that man's single! I
mean, look at him! Would you get up under him? Only time
he get laid, he gotta go the ATM.

Valdez   Eight Minutes!

Lucius   . . . Man's a damn pleasure seeker. Our pain, dass
his pleasure. Dass some Sodom and Gomorrah jazz right
there. Man ain't nuthin' but a test a faith. Ignore him.

Pause.

. . . Say, Angel . . . you ever heard that story concerning the
Mongoose and the Black-Eyed Squirrel? . . . See, there was
this Mongoose, OK? And this Mongoose – this cat was
smooth, right? Couldn't tell this Mongoose nuthin' 'bout
nuthin. Brother had it all figured, OK? Till one day, he was
out hunting for the venomous snakes, which, thass what
Mongoose do, they hunt all type a dangerous snakes,
Cobras, Asps – So, dig it: this brother's out on the hunt,
right, when here comes this little Black-eyed Squirrel? And
this squirrel, he was – how you say – he had been ousted
from his community, OK, shunned, on account a –

Angel   – I can't –

Lucius   – 'Can't'? Can't what?

Angel   I can't, I can't . . . sleep. I can't, in there, do you sleep?

Lucius   I sleep.

Angel   You breathe an' shit?

Lucius   Mostly.

Angel   . . . How?

Lucius   How? . . . Well, dass a Test a Faith too.

Angel   M-Man.

Lucius   Hey.

Angel   . . . I, I ain't made for this –

Lucius   Hey! Don't let that man see ya weak, brother.

Angel   This is fucked.

Lucius   C'mon now, son, pull it together.

Angel   I, I can't –

Lucius   Breathe! . . . You can breathe out here, can't ya? Shoot, come on now. Breathe.

Angel   Doan' wanna –

Lucius   No talkin', just breathin'! Everybody gonna make it juss fine, everybody gonna breathe and sleep. Ya breathin'?

Angel   Yeah?

Lucius   Keep doin' it then!

Angel   I, I –

Lucius   Have a cigarette, son, it'll help ya. Here, already lit, built for puffin' . . . Believe me, jack, you talkin' to a brother understands!

Angel   . . . Fuck

Lucius   Things can change, Angel. I changed. Like I said before – about the sun? – I love me some sun now, but I used ta hate the sun . . . Can ya imagine that? How's a man gonna live in Miami Beach, he don't like the sun? Shoulda moved somewhere else, I suppose, but thass a lot a work, a lot a planning. 'Where should I go?' 'What I'm goin to do when I get there?' 'Do they sell cocaine in Alaska?' Stuff like that. Too much work . . . You still breathin'?

Angel   Yeah.

Lucius   OK, so, lissen careful: there I was, Miami Beach. Paradise, right? Little apartment complex they got over there, second floor, view of the ocean, the ladies, everything . . . The ladies down there in Miami, Angel? like nobody's business, brother – awesome, incredible . . . Rent was cheap – didn't pay but four hundred bucks a month on that little place . . . Did I mention it had a little terrace? Well, it did. Never went out on it . . . Cocaine in Miami? Plentiful, jack. Extremely plentiful. And cheap. Real cheap. Dirt cheap. For all intents and purposes, the shit was free. Pardon my language, but, that's what cocaine is. Shit . . . Horseshit . . . Anyway – Oh! and Qualudes? Them, little 714s? Like takin' aspirin, baby. Take two, call me late for dinner . . . Heroin, Dilaudid? Juss pick up the phone! thirty minutes, home delivery! . . . Hated the sun though, hated it . . . I'm not talkin' 'bout 'Gee, I wish it wasn't so sunny', I'm talkin' Hate . . . Pathological Dracula Shit . . . Deep . . . Came a time, I stopped goin' in ta work if it was too sunny. Usedta call in sick, order a pizza and a twelve-pack. Pizza and a twelve-pack for 8.50, How ya gonna beat that?! Delivery boy, he was all right, little Ecuadorean kid, usedta pick me up a little somethin' on the way, a nice bag, coupla pornos, whatever I wanted, usedta blow a little smoke wit him, he'd leave happy. Nice little system. One day, he stopped by . . . I killed him. Killed him with a cowboy boot . . . I mean, I was wearin' the boot at the time, thass how I killed him . . . After I killed him, I didn't know what ta do so I chopped him up, threw him, in the dumpster, right next door. Next

door! Can ya imagine that? . . . And ya know what
happened? . . . Nuthin' . . . Not a damn thing . . . Kept
waitin' for the sirens, they never came . . . So I called up the
pizza shop, toal 'em: 'I never got my pizza.' You know what
they did? . . . They sent me another one. For free . . . Now,
to me, that's a peculiar turn of events, doncha think? . . .
Unnatural . . . I'll tell ya why I killed him . . . I killed him
'cuz he left the door open, said the place stunk, needed
some air. But when the air came in . . . the sun came with it
. . . Now . . . I think, I think that was a very unusual thing
for me to do, killing that boy, don't you? . . . Highly unusual
. . . And . . . Nuthin' happened! Nuthin' . . . One day, I
finally got up the gumption to leave Miami, but, by then, I
had killed five people . . . Five . . . Killed three more up
north, over here, but they was all white. Funny how people
start payin' attention when white people start droppin' . . .
And all a this, 'cuz I hated the sun . . . My enemy. The sun .
. . I had everything in the world down there but I didn't
have nuthin'. Now I got nuthin' but I got everythin'. I love
the sun now. Love it . . . Before? Hate. Now? Love . . . Dass
a conundrum, Kimosabee . . . When ya get back to your
cell? Doan' lie down . . . When ya can't do nuthin' else
except lie down? Then ya gonna lie down and dig on what I
juss toal' ya . . . reflect . . . Every hour, I'm a bang on my
wall three times, let ya remember you ain't alone, OK?

Angel Yeah.

Lucius Hold up, today's Monday, right?

Angel Is it?

Lucius Yeah, don't drink the soup. You'll be up all night.

Valdez *descends.*

Valdez Are there infractions goin' on over here?

Lucius No, sir.

Valdez That cigarette Droopy Dog's draggin' on, you
give it to him?

Lucius   Yes, sir.

Valdez   That would be an infraction.

Lucius   Aw c'mon, man.

Valdez   Did you just say something, Superstar?

Lucius   How's a man supposed ta know it's a infraction to give another man a cigarette, when there ain't never was no other man here 'cept me till now?!

Valdez   You didn't read the manual?

Lucius   'The manual'?!

Valdez   The manual states quite clearly –

Lucius   Fuck your damn manual!

Valdez   Take a day off from the yard, both of you, so you can reflect on infractions.

Lucius   Bullshit, mothahfuckah!

Valdez   Two days!

Lucius   I'm gonna –

Valdez   A week! . . . Perhaps your 'higher entity' can sort this out for you . . . Cruz!!!

Angel   I didn't say nuttin' –

Valdez   They releasing you.

Angel   They are?

Valdez   Just kidding . . . Away from your cages, girls, let's go.

Crossfade.

Act Two

Scene One

The yard, days later. **Mary Jane** *speaks.*

Mary Jane On the first day of Angel's trial, I had a
headache, a backache, I hadn't slept in over forty-eight
hours, and I was staring at a mountain of compelling
evidence pointed squarely against my case. I never felt
better. The DA had so much evidence and so many
eyewitnesses to work with, he knew he couldn't lose. Every
piece of evidence, I found a way to cast the slimmest shadow
of doubt. And his witnesses? They were all church members.
I buried them one after the other. In court, I constantly had
to suppress the urge to smile. On November 18th, the DA
invited me for dinner and drinks at Patsy's. I knew what was
coming. He offered Angel this: plead to manslaughter, he'd
recommend the minimum sentence, Angel does eight years,
everybody wins. I turned him down flat. He told me to talk
it over with Angel, and get back to him in the morning. The
next morning I told him: 'Sorry, no deal.' I never consulted
Angel in the matter, never even mentioned it. I knew I had
a win . . . I did make two mistakes. When I turned down the
DA's offer of a deal that morning, I was not humble, and I
did not suppress my smile. The second mistake was: I had
overlooked a prosecution eyewitness who was on the list to
testify. He was a British PhD candidate doing his thesis on
Living Religions who had been at the church that night. I
assumed he was some kinda bearded flake from the land of
Academia, but he wasn't. He was clean-cut, credible and,
amazingly, had experience as a witness. He corroborated all
the previous testimony of all the previous witnesses who I
had previously discredited and I couldn't shake him up. In a
moment of weakness, I went to the DA, looking for a deal,
which of course, 'Fuck you, bitch!' . . . 'Fuck you, bitch' –
well, OK, fine – but that still didn't change the fact that
Angel did not intend to cause Reverend Kim's death. This

was not first-degree murder. The law may not have seen it that way, but the fact is: the law is fallible. Angel had tried every means at his disposal to bring back his friend. And when everything failed, he still didn't give up. He made a foolish, perilous statement, but, it was a statement. I find honor in that. I wanted to find honor in myself. And so I did. And it was right – Goddamnit, it was right.

Crossfade.

Lucius (*to* **Angel**)   Long time no see, brother. How'd Cruel and Unusual Punishment treat ya?

Valdez (*from his post*)   I heard that!

Lucius   Wit all due respect, Valdez, if it's a infraction to breathe God's air, juss tell us now and we'll asphyxiate ourselves.

Angel   Yo, doan' start no shit –

Lucius   That man ain't nuttin' but a apparition! (*For* **Valdez**.) An' we gonna conversate about whatever strikes our damn amusement, believe that! Maybe we gonna speak on the mating habits of the Yella-Bellied Sap Suckah; maybe we'll conduct a symposium on some Butterscotch Puddin'!

Angel   Yo, bro –

Lucius   Hey Valdez! ACLU's a fine institution, ain't it?

Angel   ACLU?

Lucius (*to* **Angel**)   You think we back out here early cuz 'Ol Valdez is tender hearted? (*Miming being on the phone.*) Hey, Valdez! My lawyer's on the phone, it's for you! . . . Ha! . . . Want me ta tell him you in the shower soapin' up your privates? . . . Ah, what's a matter, brother: Constitution got your tongue? . . . Ha! . . . (*Phone.*) 'Now what's that, Mr Cooperstein? . . . Yes, sir, I'll be sure to tell him . . . No, no, quite all right. You have a nice day too, Mr C.' . . . Hey, Valdez! Mr C say to remind ya that we could talk about anything under the sun 'cept for conspiracy and treason, and if ya got a problem wit dat, he say he got a cousin owns a Dairy Queen, could prolly get you a job flippin' burgers or sweepin' up.

Valdez   Fifty-four minutes!

Lucius   God loves ya, Valdez, ya know that right?! He loves ya and He gonna leave the light on for ya too, always does! God love ya so much, even makes me wanna love ya, in fact, I do love ya! Angel love ya too, ain't that right, Angel?! We love ya 'cuz God love ya, And make no mistake, soldier, God, Jesus, Jehovah, Yahweh, the Holy Ghost, they L-O-V-E-Y-O-U, praise be! Ha!

Valdez *enters.*

Valdez   Do you believe in God, Cruz?

Angel   What?

Valdez   You heard me.

Angel   I, uh – yo, this ain't got nuthin to do wit' me.

Lucius   It's OK, son, tell the man.

Angel   Look –

Valdez   It's a simple question, Droopy Dog.

Angel   I ain't fuckin' Droopy Dog!

Valdez   Then answer the question! Do you believe in God?

Angel   . . . Dass my business.

Valdez   It's funny. Some people, they got big balls when they're high on narcotics, brandishing weapons, killing a man, but take away the drugs and the guns, ask them a simple question, and what happens? They revert back to what they really are, ain't that right, Droopy Dog?

Lucius   Someone need ta give you a hug, Valdez.

Valdez   If there's a God, Superstar, you ain't never gonna
meet him! Very soon, Mr Superstar, very soon, you gonna
be flyin' the Friendly Skies. All your lawyers, and your
notoriety, and your delusions of grandeur, they all add up to
zip. You are a defect of evolution like a three-legged dog,
and when you get to Florida, they gonna put you down!

Lucius   That makes ya happy, don't it?

Valdez   Happy? Why should I be happy? They gonna
feed you lobster, strap you down, put you outta your misery.
What's happy about that? No. What makes me happy is
lookin' at you right now and seeing the sheer terror in your
eyes. Because that terror will haunt you every day until the
State of Florida relieves it with a lethal injection! And that
terror, along with whatever misery I can provide, is the only
justice that the families of your victims are ever gonna get!

Lucius   I'm a pray for you, man.

Valdez   Then pray . . . Me? I'm feeling a bit parched; I
think I need a beverage. And being a free man, I think I'll
run down to the staff cafeteria and choose from a wide
assortment of refreshing drinks. Perhaps I'll purchase a Kit-
Kat and a Bear Claw, something to tide me over 'til I leave
here and go eat whatever I want for dinner.

Lucius   Hope you're monitoring your cholesterol –

Valdez   – What?!

Lucius   Wouldn't want ya ta drop dead before you've
been saved.

Valdez   'Saved'?! I am a good man because I choose to
be! End of story! Not because I fear God. Not because I
wanna go to some Holy Playground when I kick the bucket!
I go to work, I pay my taxes, I observe the law. I didn't kill
eight people! I don't need to be 'saved'! Do you really
believe that there's a thing called God? . . . Or is it that your
pain is so unbearable that you force yourself to create a
belief in order to medicate that pain? . . . And, if there is a

God, Superstar, do you honestly believe that you are free
from the burden of what you've done?! . . . And if there isn't
a God, then what are you really? 'Cuz in a meaningless
existence, your only function was to be a source of pain and
death, like cancer or a plane crash! You renounced your
humanity when you claimed your first victim! Now what are
you? I think you know, Superstar. I look at you, and I know
that you know! And the most compassionate advice I can
give you is this: when you get back to your cell, bang your
head against the wall until your brains spill out, only, please,
do it after six so I don't have ta clean the shit up! . . . Now I
will be back . . . shortly!

Valdez *exits.*

Pause.

Angel   Yo, doan' lissen to that, mothahfuckah, he don't
know shit.

Lucius   . . . I know.

Angel   Man's a fuckin' asshole.

Lucius   Misguided.

Pause.

Angel   You think the sun's gonna come out before our
time's up?

Lucius   You don't believe in God, huh?

Angel   I didn't say that.

Lucius   God said to Peter: 'Before this night is through,
you gonna deny me three times.' Peter say: 'Not me, Lord, I
could never deny you.' Then dawn came, the cock done
crowed, and Peter had denied his Lord three times on the
night a his arrest.

Angel   I know that story –

Lucius   – When Jesus died on the cross, you know who
was there wit' him? I ain't talkin' 'bout Roman soldiers and

the blasphemin' crowd, I'm talkin 'bout: who was there for
him? I'll tell ya who was there. His mother, Mary
Magdalene, 'coupla aunts, and some streetwalkin' ho's. All
women. The twelve apostles? Hiding in fear. His pops, St
Joseph? He was at the bar talkin' 'bout 'Pour me another
wine, Lazarus'. It was the women showed up for Jesus.
Matthew, Mark, Luke and John, them cats had time ta
make up for their sins, how much time I got? Thass why I'm
a speak my mind! Thass why I ain't gonna let no
mustachioed Roman soldier squelch my positive self-
expression! Every day I got left, I'm a live free. I'm a open
up that gift God give me each and every day, save me the
wrappin' paper so's I could package up my gift and pass it
on. Ain't gonna live in fear no more! I'm a show up for Jesus
like he showed up for me!

Angel   You want a cigarette, man?

Lucius   Them things'll kill ya, brother. Now, how is it you
ain't a believer?

Angel   Look, man, this ain't a conversation you wanna
have with me.

Lucius   Some of the greatest saints, they was non-
believers, having the crisis of faith right up to the end.

Angel   I'm not havin' a crisis.

Lucius   Lemme pose to you a little hypothetical, brother:
. . . what if God existed?

Angel   I really ain't up for this, bro.

Lucius   Lemme juss kick it like this then, shortpants: if I
were ta say to you, today, that God not only exists, but has a
plan for ya, brother, that you are here, right here and now,
because God planned for this to be, truly, the first day of the
rest of your life –

Angel   Yo, man –

Lucius   Hear me out: if I said that the life you will live from this day forward will be happy, joyous and free, and with Divine Purpose –

Angel   Juror number one, she likes me.

Lucius   What?!

Angel   I'm sayin: In my trial, I think that juror number one likes me.

Lucius   Yeah, well, so long as jurors number two through twelve like you too, then you got no problem, but in the mean-time –

Angel   Nah, man, I mean, she likes me.

Lucius   Yeah, so what?

Angel   I'm juss sayin she likes me, what's wrong wit dat?

Lucius   Don't you take no disputatious attitude on me –

Angel   What's wrong with juror number one wanting to get with me?

Lucius   Get with you?! Well, hey now, Casanova, that's very special, I'm happy for ya, but I'm a tell you right now, either you got your signals crossed or that female is emotionally disturbed –

Angel   'Cuz she likes me?

Lucius   What kinda church-goin' woman gonna make goo-goo eyes at some criminal defendant?

Angel   Why she gotta be a 'church-goin' woman'? Why can't she juss be a woman, like, she's a woman and I'm a man?

Lucius   Oh, you think you a man, huh?

Angel   I'm juss sayin' she likes me.

Lucius   I bet she's fat.

Angel   She ain't fat, man.

Lucius   You seen her standing up? . . . I rest my case.

Angel   Yo, juss 'cuz you ain't got no woman –

Lucius   I gotta woman! And she's called the Virgin Mary, Mother of God, and she's a source of comfort and understanding, a solace in a sea of turpitude!

Angel   Yeah, well, juror number one ain't fat.

Lucius   She go to Jenny Craig, believe that! I seen 'em all!

Angel   Whatchu seen lately to be the judge a anything?

Lucius   I see a fool standin' before me, tell ya that for free. I see all I need to see. Don't ya get my dander up now, son. Don't you danderize me! And don't you never change the subject on me again when I'm pursuin' a line of thought like I was subsequent to your pointless little interruption. Talkin' about girls? Shoot. You see any girls here?

Angel   I'm juss sayin' –

Lucius   Say! Say! Say! What I'm sayin' is: if you horny, go in the corner and whack your pee-pee, juss leave me out of it.

Angel   And I'm sayin': I ain't interested in any conversation about God.

Lucius   You don't like God?

Angel   I didn't say that.

Lucius   I'm not saying that you did. I'm asking you a question, a direct question: do you like God?

Angel   I don't know God, OK? You know him, or you think you know him –

Lucius   Think I know him?

Angel   Whatever, you know him –

Lucius   – No, no, no, son. It's not 'whatever'. Either I know him or I don't. What do you think? Do I know him?

Angel   I don't know –

Lucius   – 'Don't know'?! Don't try to jive me with 'You don't know'. Of course you know! You juss' too feeble-hearted and trifling to lissen to what you already know to be true in your damaged heart! I look like a fool to you?

Angel   It ain't like that, man –

Lucius   – Or maybe you juss' think I'm insane, 'Black Plague', 'Boogie Man', 'Boo Mothahfuckah! Comin to eat you up!' That it? You think I'm some kinda cancerous plane crash?

Angel   You're cool, man, you're cool –

Lucius   – Cool?! You lucky they got a cage between us, talkin' 'bout 'cool'! Be anything you wanna be in this life, son, be a damn 'atheist, arsonist, lowlife, heretic, Antichrist, politician, cable TV installer', any kinda general miscreant tickles your T-bone, but doncha ever be cool! And doncha ever try to tell me that I'm cool, 'cuz I juss' won't stand for it! Be Blazin' or Be Freezin', but doncha ever be cool! Cool?! Shit! That's juss a waste of my time, and I care about my damn time! Do you hear me? . . . I said: do you hear me?

Angel   I'm, I'm sorry –

Lucius   I didn't ask you were you sorry. I take one look at you and I can tell you frankly, you one of the sorriest people I ever seen. I asked you: Do You Hear Me?

Angel   I hear you.

Lucius   Do you hear me?

Angel   I ain't the fuckin' enemy, man.

Lucius   You need to inspect yourself, so you can respect yourself, little man!

Angel   You know what? Why don'chu juss' inspect your fuckin' self, motherfuckah.

Lucius   You need ta get straight wit' the Lord, pancho.

Angel   You straight with the Lord, Lucius?!

Lucius   August 4th, 1996, I was out here at night, dark night, black . . . Before I knew it, the sky filled wit' light, some kinda meteor shower, eclipse, somethin, out a nowhere I felt God! No rational explanation 'cept I felt Him. Felt His light. Powerful light! And on my knees, I begged His mercy and forgiveness! And the funny thing is, I had felt it before, that feeling. A few times. But I never attributed it ta God. I always thought, when it happened: 'It's the smack, or the cocaine, some kinda deja-who' – wasn't none of that! God had touched me, but I juss thought it was the wind . . . God forgives me for what I done, and He'll forgive you too if 'ya ask Him.

Angel   You ain't straight wit' shit.

Lucius   And you know that how?

Angel   Doan' make me fuckin' hurt you, man.

Lucius   Hurt me? How a little chihuahua like you gonna harm me?

Angel   You could call me fuckin' names, talk down to me like I'm some fuckin' schoolkid, it don't change the facts!

Lucius   Curse, curse, curse! Chirp! Chirp! Chirp! That's what you is– a little dumb sparrow, chirpin' in the wind!

Angel   Valdez was right about you.

Lucius   Chirp, chirp, chirp –

Angel   You killed eight people, man. You a damn psychopath! A fuckin' nut job, talkin' 'bout God, talkin' 'bout Kingdom of Heaven; you can talk shit all you want, say your prayers twenty-four hours a day, it don't mean shit!

Lucius   Doan' mean shit, huh?

Angel   Dass right.

Lucius   Prayer doan' mean shit?

Angel   You deaf, motherfuckah, thass what I said!

Lucius   If prayer doan' mean shit, then how come I was awoken the other night to hear a sorry little bitch stutterin' over some prayer in between chokes 'n' sobs 'n' snorts from inhaling the little puddle a tears on his damp little prison pillow? . . . If prayer doan' mean shit, then what the fuck were you doing Tuesday last? Or Monday? Or lass Saturday after lunch, for that matter? 'Cuz I don't think it was Valdez I heard, and you the onlyest motherfuckah up in here besides me. So, do prayer mean shit, or don't it? You tell me . . .

Angel   It's a habit, dass all.

Lucius   That ain't no habit. Cocaine, dass a habit! What you was doin' was somethin else . . . Know what I think? I think you need to stand up right now and open your heart to Jesus. That pain and anguish and sadness inside ya, it ain't leavin' by its own volition. It got a nice home inside a you rent free! Why the fuck it gonna leave without being kicked out? It's time to serve them motherfuckahs their eviction papers, Angel! It's time to liberate the profound and genteel man that is you. This prison, these cages, they ain't shit, brother! Inside my heart and my mind, I am sailing on the Pacific on a fine schooner basking in the light of life. You ever been to the Pacific Ocean. It's real nice, Angel –

Angel   – Dat ship you floatin' on, it ain't made a nothin', Lucius.

Lucius   Ain't sprung a leak in nearly two years, day I found God, right where you standin'.

Angel   And you don't think that's juss a little bit convenient?

Lucius   Oh, it's convenient! Who tryin' ta say it ain't convenient?

Angel   I'm talkin' 'bout findin' God in prison.

Lucius   Any place where you can have your life resurrected, thass a damn convenient place.

Angel   After you killed eight people –

Lucius   Thass between me and God.

Angel   And thass very convenient too!

Lucius   Well, God juss happens to be a very damn convenient individual, brother! I coulda had God when I was six, sixteen, thirty-two, thirty-five, he wasn't goin' nowhere! It happens I didn't get him 'till I was forty-two; a suicidal, multiple homicidal drug addict starin' down at death row! Would I have preferred to find him at twenty-five? Hell, yeah! But I didn't! Now why's everyone wanna turn and blame God for that?

Angel   Ain't no one blamin' God here. You killed those people, not God.

Lucius   I ain't never said I didn't.

Angel   I doan wanna talk about this!

Lucius   What'd you do to get in here anyway?

Angel   Dass my business.

Lucius   I know what you did. I seent it on the TV. You killed a man.

Angel   I didn't kill him!

Lucius   Now how's that?

Angel   Worry 'bout your own shit!

Lucius   You killed him.

Angel   No I didn't!

Lucius   Man's dead, ain't he?

Angel   I juss shot him in the ass.

Lucius   And then what happened?

Angel   Fuck you mean, 'Then what happened?' He fell down, screamin' like a little bitch, they grabbed me –

Lucius   What happened to him?

Angel   He went to the hospital –

Lucius   Then what happened?

Angel   They made a operation on his ass, he was fine –

Lucius   – 'Fine'?

Angel   I juss' shot him in the fuckin' ass!

Lucius   Then how'd he end up dead, jack?

Angel   Doctors! Fuckin Medical Malpractice! Shit, what's so fuckin' hard 'bout takin' a bullet out a mothahfuckah's ass? Ya take a knife, a fuckin' scalpel, whatever, ya open the ass, ya find the shit. What's the 'complication' 'bout that? 'Complication'?! Juss open up the ass, whatever's not 'ass', take the shit out! How's it my fault some drunk mothahfuckah can't tell the difference between a bullet and a man's ass?!

Lucius   So the doctor was drunk?

Angel   Prolly! You know how them mothahfuckahs be!

Lucius   So, how'd the man die then?

Angel   Like I said, 'complication'! First doctor – mo-fuckin' Dr Dolittle – he obviously ain't did the job right, they had ta bring the mothahfuckah back, put him on the operatin' table, 'simple procedure', but the mothahfuckah dies!

Lucius   Die from what?

Angel   Heart attack! How the fuck? I mean, this mothahfuckah, Reverend Kim, he say he the Son a God! How's a real Son a God gonna let himself go out like that?! 'Cuz if I was God, and I sent my son down here to do a job, and he came back talkin' 'bout 'Yeah, Pop, they shot my ass, and, my heart, it juss couldn't take it', (?!), I'd slap the mothahfuckah upside his head! I'd tell him: 'You better look in the mirror, kid; now I gotta send your sister down to do a man's job!' Mothahfuckah oughta be ashamed of himself! They hung Jesus from a cross! Banged nails into his feet and hands –

Lucius   But you ain't shot Jesus', ass, did ya?

Angel   Hell, no!

Lucius   You shot a man.

Angel   And I'd do it again.

Lucius   Not the Son a God, a man. Man died.

Angel   And dass my fault?!

Lucius   Did you shoot a man?

Angel   Get the fuck out my face.

Lucius   Did he die?

Angel   Not 'cuz a me!

Lucius   If ya didn't shoot him, would he be dead now?

Angel   You killed eight people, mothahfuckah! Who you talkin to?

Lucius   You shot a man. The man died. Ain't no man no more.

Angel   But –

Lucius   But what? Dead is dead, son, I know you know that.

Angel   It's not my fault.

Lucius   Meaning what?

Angel   Meaning it ain't my fuckin' fault!

Lucius   Now that's juss plain illogical. That's like me tellin' you dat a hippopotamus knows howta fry himself some eggs.

Angel   That man deserved to die.

Lucius   No human man deserves ta die!

Angel   Why, cuz 'God' say so?

Lucius   Dass right.

Angel   When exactly did 'God' say that shit?

Lucius   Bible say –

Angel   Fuck the Bible! Bible ain't no autobiography, man! 'God' didn't write the shit! Buncha mothahfuckahs wrote that shit. Apostles didn't write no Gospel, and Jesus, that mothahfuckah, never wrote one damn word! Not even a fuckin' postcard! Dass a fact! Ain't my fault the man died, but he dead now, so what? He juss one man outta a billion, people die every day.

Lucius   Ain't murdered every day.

Angel   Nah, they gotta run into you first to earn dat distinction.

Lucius   Or you!

Angel   I did somethin' had to be done!

Lucius   Then accept it then! You man enough to do it, then, be man enough ta stand behind it! But you can't really stand behind it, 'cuz you know it's wrong! You know it!

Angel   Do you know it's wrong ta kill a man?

Lucius   Course I do.

Angel   Then why you got lawyers fightin' extradition for you?

Lucius   I'm gonna do 'life' here in New York State anyway! I pled guilty. I took responsibility! Why I gotta go to a place where they tryin to kill me?

Angel   I thought you was straight wit' God, man?

Lucius   I am.

Angel   If you straight, then why you gotta fear death, mothahfuckah? Alls you gotta do is die, then, you gonna be in heaven wit' 'God', right?! Ain't that the ultimate goal? If that shit is true like you say, then what's the fuckin' problem then? God forgives you, right? You juss stood there in my face an toal' me that shit. So what's the dilly, yo?! . . . You try to tell me you floatin' on the Pacific wit' your sailor cap on?! Dass bullshit! You don't act like no inner-peace mothahfuckah I ever met! You act angry and crazy.

Lucius   I'm in prison, Jack!

Angel   You killed eight people yo, your ass should be in prison! Tell me: 'Be a man'! Why doan' you be a man, go die like ya supposed to? You gots the God insurance, what else you need?

Lucius   Ain't got no more time ta waste on imbeciles –

Angel   You afraid ta die cuz your ass know only two things gonna happen when you do die: either nuthin', or somethin' bad! Ain't no God, ain't no light!

Valdez *enters.*

Valdez   Peanut chew!

Angel   Take me outta here, Valdez!

Valdez   Away from the cage, convict.

Valdez *enters cage, cuffs* **Angel**.

Angel   I ain't no convict!

Valdez   Not yet.

Angel   Not yet, not ever!

Valdez   Dat ain't what I hear.

Angel   Never!

Lucius   Spittin' in the wind, son!

Angel   Rather spit in it than lissen to it!

Lucius   'You could cast out the devil, but ya can't cast out God!'

Angel   I ain't got God and neither do you.

Lucius   I'm a perfect child a God and so are you. He got a plan for us all! Valdez too!

Angel   Hurry up and die, mothahfuckah!

Valdez   . . . You know what, Droopy Dog? I'm beginning to like you.

Scene Two

Visitations area. Riker's Island. Two days later.

Mary Jane   'God's fucking Plan'?!

Angel   I'm juss sayin' –

Mary Jane   Saying what?! That God's plan is: you should spend the rest of your life in prison?! What kinda plan is that?! It's the district attorney's plan, Angel, that's whose plan it is, not 'God's'! What is wrong with you?!

Angel   I didn't say I believed the shit.

Mary Jane   Well, hey – how very skeptical of you!

Angel   I think Lucius was juss –

Mary Jane   'Lucius'?! What, You're on a first-name basis now?!

Angel   I see the mothahfuckah every day. He the only one I got up there –

Mary Jane   Oh, well then, by all means, mingle! Mingle with the deranged psychotic serial killer!

Angel   See, he ain't really like that –

Mary Jane   What?!

Angel   I know –

Mary Jane   Do you have any idea who Lucius Jenkins is?!

Angel   I know, he killed eight people, right?

Mary Jane   Eight that we know of!

Angel   He told me eight.

Mary Jane   So what 'He told you eight'?! What does that mean?! 'Case closed, Lucius told Angel eight'?! And what, eight's not enough for you?!

Angel   I hear you, all right? Let's juss' get back ta business.

Mary Jane   Maybe Lucius should be your lawyer!

Angel   Yo, I was juss' makin' conversation –

Mary Jane   When you're acquitted, Angel, when we're sitting in a bar together drinking beer and eating chicken wings, then make conversation! Unless you wanna just have a conversation now, exchange recipes, talk philosophy, forget the whole thing!

Angel   You tryin' ta back out now?!

Mary Jane   Are you?

Angel   Yo, I'm here, Mary Jane.

Mary Jane   I am putting my career on the line for you, Angel, my vocation! So you better be damn sure your head's screwed back on before I even think about putting you on that witness stand and suborning perjury!

Angel   I'm down wit' the program and I'm gonna thank you 'till my dyin' day, believe me.

Mary Jane   I could lose my license! They could toss me in jail!

Angel   I'm already in jail and I'm gonna get out any way I can, swear ta God!

Mary Jane   DA asks you a question, what do you do?

Angel   Pause five seconds.

Mary Jane   Then what?

Angel   Answer the shit.

Mary Jane   Answer how?

Angel   'Yes', 'No', or 'I don't know'.

Mary Jane   And then what?

Angel   Stop.

Mary Jane   Stop what?

Angel   Stop talking.

Mary Jane   Why?

Angel   'Cuz I might say some shit I shouldn't say.

Mary Jane   What if it needs to be said?

Angel   I don't know –

Mary Jane   Do you wanna spend the rest of your life in prison?!

Angel   Whadda you think?

Mary Jane   I don't know, Angel! What should I think?

Angel   I wanna get the fuck outta here.

Mary Jane   God won't have a problem with that?

Angel   Ask fuckin' God.

Mary Jane   I'm asking you.

Angel   Fuck God! He ain't got nuthin' to do wit' this.

Mary Jane   How do you know that?

Angel   I don't know –

Mary Jane   – I can't work with 'I don't know'! If I'm gonna put you on the stand and risk my job, then I need to know that you know!

Angel   I know.

Mary Jane   No, you don't.

Angel   I do know, really, truss me –

Mary Jane   It's not about trust –

Angel   Aaight, look: that mothahfuckah Reverend Kim, he was a false prophet, fuckin' heretic, cashed in on God's name, fucked up not just Joey, but a lot a fuckin' people, right?! God should understand why I brought the mothahfuckah down, and if He don't, then . . . fuck Him! I'm juss a ordinary man, I ain't no martyr, and if that's God's plan for me, then you know what? Fuck the damn plan! And thass how I know, all right?!

Mary Jane   You gotta problem with lying?

Angel   I love to lie, tell me what to say.

Mary Jane   Tell me a lie.

Angel   About what?

Mary Jane   Anything. Lie. Right now.

Angel   Aaight . . . I invented electricity.

Mary Jane   Stop messing around!

Angel   I ain't messin' around. I invented the shit!

Mary Jane   Do you know how electricity works?

Angel   Not exactly.

Mary Jane   Then that's a dumb lie! Tell me a smart lie.

Angel   Like what?

Mary Jane   My father drank Jameson's.

Angel   Dass a lie?

Mary Jane   He drank Bushmill's. But it's a smart lie because my father was a first generation Irish Catholic who supported the IRA and Bushmill's is known as a Protestant whiskey because it comes from the North. So it would be logical to assume that he wouldn't be caught dead drinking a Protestant whiskey, even though he did. That's a lie built on truth. That's why it's a good lie. Because it's true. Now, tell me a true lie, Angel.

Angel   Aaight . . . I tried ta kill Reverend Kim that night.

Mary Jane   What?!

Angel   I mean, it's a lie 'cuz, I didn't try ta kill him, but it's true 'cuz . . .

Mary Jane   Because what?

Angel   It's true 'cuz . . . 'cuz it kinda makes sense that I might have wanted to, right?

Mary Jane   I'm the DA, you're you: 'Did you shoot Reverend Kim?'

Angel   . . . No.

Mary Jane   Look me in the eye when you say it. 'Did you shoot him?'

Angel   No.

Mary Jane   You're lying!

Angel   Whaddya want me to do, say 'yes'?

Mary Jane   I want you to believe what you're saying.

Angel   But it ain't true.

Mary Jane   Make it true! 'Did you shoot him?'

Angel   No.

Mary Jane   Why can you say that?

Angel   I don't know.

Mary Jane   Think about it.

Angel   ... 'Cuz ... I ain't like that?

Mary Jane   Why not?

Angel   It ain't in me.

Mary Jane   Why not?

Angel   I'm not, you know –

Mary Jane   – No, I don't. You're not what?

Angel   I'm like, guns scare me.

Mary Jane   Guns scare everyone.

Angel   Nah, I mean, like, holding one.

Mary Jane   Why's that?

Angel   'Cuz a somethin that happened once –

Mary Jane   – So it would make sense to you that you would never hold a gun again?

Angel   Yeah.

Mary Jane   OK. 'Did you bring a gun to the church that night?'

Angel   ... Nah.

Mary Jane   Say 'No'.

Angel   No.

Mary Jane   Good. Now why would it make sense to you that you wouldn't shoot Reverend Kim?

Angel   'Cuz it's wrong?

Mary Jane   What's wrong?

Angel   Shootin' someone.

Mary Jane   Fair enough. 'Did you shoot Reverend Kim?'

Angel   No.

Mary Jane   'You shot him, didn't you?'

Angel   No.

Mary Jane   'Did you ever think about hurting Reverend Kim?'

Angel   No.

Mary Jane   Say yes to that.

Angel   Why?

Mary Jane   Because you only have to lie twice: when he asks you if you had a gun on you, and when he asks you if you shot Kim. Everything else, tell the truth.

Angel   It won't make me look bad?

Mary Jane   It will make you look truthful . . . The jury wants to acquit you, Angel. They just need to hear you say sincerely and believably that you didn't do it, and they will clear you.

Angel   And they could do that?

Mary Jane   It's called Jury Annulment. Even if it was totally obvious that you did it, the jury can refuse to convict, and that's it. End of story.

Angel   And no one can say shit?

Mary Jane   No one.

Angel   Even though it's wrong?

Mary Jane   You think what you did is wrong?

Angel   You mean, technically?

Mary Jane   Last month you didn't think you did anything wrong!

Angel   I ain't sayin' it's wrong, but, technically, the truth is: I shot him, right? Technically, thass kinda wrong, isn't it?

Mary Jane   What are you saying, Angel?

Angel   I mean, what do you think about it?

Mary Jane   It doesn't matter what I think.

Angel   What if I said that it mattered to me?

Mary Jane   Do you wanna stop the trial, plead guilty?

Angel   I wanna know what you think.

Mary Jane   Our jury, Angel, they want to acquit you because it's right, not because it's wrong. They don't think you deserve 'life' or anything close to it. No one blames you for Reverend Kim's death except the State of New York! And what is that? It's an institution! It's a set of rules set up to apply to each and every circumstance, as if they're all the same. They are not all the same. The jury knows that. And they will clear you of all charges, from murder on down, because they understand what happened here beyond the 'technicalities' and they empathize. Not because of your dazzling smile, but because, under the same circumstances as you, they might have done the same damn thing themselves. You made a statement, Angel. And they are going to back that statement up. Your testimony will supply reasonable doubt. And that's all they want. And that's what I think. Make sense?

Angel   . . . Huh?

Mary Jane   Does it make sense to you?

Angel   Oh . . . Yeah . . . Yeah.

Mary Jane   Are you sure?

Angel   I was juss –

Mary Jane   Just what?

Angel   . . . Thinking

Mary Jane   About what?

Angel   . . . Joey.

Mary Jane   . . . Oh.

Angel   . . . We usta, me and Joey, we usta sneak out our house on Sunday nights, jump the turnstiles. And we would hop down onto the subway tracks, walk through the tunnels, lookin' for shit, makin' adventures, playin' like we was GI Joes . . .

Pick up a empty can a Hawaiian Punch or some ol' beer bottle for fake walkie-talkies, . . . and we'd have our snow-boots on so we could be astronauts. And we would pretend we were the last two survivors on earth and that we came from the future . . . (stupid) . . . the future . . . like in that *Planet of the Apes* movie with the two guys? Only we had no weapons, juss Chocolate Milk . . . And we'd get so lost in our games and our discoveries, and our made-up stories . . . so many stories: lookin' for ghosts, lookin' for apes, lookin' for fortunes, runnin' from rats, talkin' 'bout girls, talkin' 'bout Thelma from 'Good Times', talkin' 'bout daydreams, talkin' 'bout Bruce Lee versus Evil Knievil, talkin' in words that wasn't even words, . . . and . . . and it would always surprise us when we saw the Lights, . . . even though we could feel the train coming, but it was the Lights . . . The closer those lights came, rumble of the tracks, sound a the conductor's horn blarin' at us, We'd get so excited we'd freeze – two seconds of freezin' cold . . . hypnotized . . . holdin' hands, waitin', waitin', then: bang . . . We'd jump off the rails, hug the wall, climb back up the platform, start runnin' – runnin' – tearin' ass clear across town back to Riverside or Cherry Park . . . One time . . . one particular time, when we was holdin' hands right before we jumped off the rails, somethin' happened, and we couldn't let go, couldn't untangle ourself from each other, and we were inside that Light, and . . . we both saw skeletons and radiation, and we was paralyzed in a way that I juss' can't explain, till somethin' blew us apart, juss' blew us, and we

landed safe . . . We didn't move for a long time . . . We was
cryin', and Joey ripped his brother's coat . . . We wasn't
speakin' till we got to our block and Joey said that it was the
Light that ripped us apart and saved our lives . . . Joey said,
'Jesus hopped the "A" train to see us safe to bed' . . .

Mary Jane   . . . Do you believe that?

Angel   . . . We was juss kids.

Mary Jane   Yeah . . . Well, you're on an 'A' train right
now, Angel, and if there's a Jesus on board it's me.

Angel   I know.

Mary Jane   DA asks you a question?

Angel   Pause five seconds.

Mary Jane   And then?

Angel   Answer it.

Mary Jane   How?

Angel   'Yes', 'No', 'I don't know'.

Mary Jane   And then?

Angel   Stop talking.

Mary Jane   Because?

Angel   He gonna try ta fuck me up.

Mary Jane   If you want to explain something?

Angel   You'll ask me in the re-direct.

Mary Jane   Did you bring a gun to the church?

Angel   No.

Mary Jane   Did you shoot Reverend Kim?

Angel   No.

Mary Jane   Did you ever want to hurt him?

Angel   Yes.

Mary Jane   What's God's plan for you?

Angel   Chicken wings and beer.

Mary Jane   All right, let's get back to work.

Scene Three

Charlie D'Amico *speaks.*

D'Amico   Lucius Jenkins was executed by the State of Florida on June 3rd . . . Me and the wife, Mary, we took a plane down to Tallahassee to be there for Lou since he didn't really have nobody except a sister in East St Louis who couldn't attend because of somethin' or other. I didn't get to talk to Lou or nothin', we were just permitted to witness the death . . . It was quick . . . The thing that freaked me out the most was they had this clock on the wall in the room where Lucius was. It was hangin' right above the hospital gurney and it said 'Standard' on it, juss' like the clocks we had at Riker's. I kept starin' at that clock and at the little red hand goin' around marking the minutes and the big black hand clickin' them off. I felt like I could hear it clickin' through the plexi-glass. I kept thinkin' how I'd stare at that same clock at work wanting it to move faster, and now here I was in Florida wishin' it could move slower or just stop. I hated that clock mostly 'cuz I felt it was fuckin' redundant . . . When they brought Lou in, he was silent. He didn't ever say nuthin', which surprised me. The only thing he said was, they asked him if he had a final statement to make and he said: 'No, sir.' . . . He only looked out at us once. He looked right at me and I tried ta smile but it was like he didn't recognize me, and for like a split second I was pissed; I was thinkin': 'This trip cost us like a thousand bucks, at least he could acknowledge our fuckin' presence, ya know?' . . . It's crazy, but that's really what I thought. I guess people don't stop being people just because something deep is goin' on. My wife Mary had just the right expression on her face though, and she cried real, real quietly, so as not to upset the families or take away from the thing that was happenin' right in front of us . . . I tried real hard to figure out what he was feelin' or thinkin', but it was real hard to tell from lookin' at him. It almost looked as if he wasn't feelin' nuthin'; and I thought I knew him too well to believe that that could really be the case, but . . . I was wrong. It turns out Lucius musta found himself another Oreo cookie man, 'cuz when the coroner did a toxicology on him, they found substantial traces of heroin and cocaine in the bloodstream. Lucius, died high as a kite . . . When it was over, me and Mary went to this diner across the street from our motel that advertised itself as having 'Tallahassee's Finest Southern Fried Chicken'. We ordered two plates, and when the waitress brought it over, we got all excited 'cuz it looked so big and juicy and plump, but when I stuck my fork into this big plump fried chicken, it deflated like a balloon . . . We got the check, went back to the motel, ordered a pizza from Domino's, called my sister-in-law so we could talk to the kids. When we got off the phone, Mary kissed me – like she really meant it. I kissed her back, and we went to bed and made love for the first time in six months . . . When the pizza guy came, we pretended we weren't there . . . I could tell you that Lucius Jenkins helped me stop drinkin' 'cuz he did, that he convinced me to look into startin' a pool-cleaning business wit' my brother-in-law, which we also did, and that he got me fired off my job which turned out to be a huge blessin' in disguise; and that stuff is all important and true, but really, I only knew the guy for three months, which ain't a lot, and if someone were ta say that he just used me or whatever, that he was a lunatic, I prolly couldn't argue back much. Ask me about drinkin' and jails, I'll tell ya a lot. Ask me about pool cleanin', I'll take my chances against anybody. Ask me about Lucius Jenkins, there ain't a hell of a lot I can say 'cuz there ain't a hell of a lot I know.

All I really know about Lucius Jenkins is that I liked him.

Scene Four

The yard, the next day, midstream.

Angel   – Yo, why ya gotta be a little bitch for? C'mon,
man! Lucius . . . Yo, Lucius . . . You stupid, man . . . You
actin' like – you know who you actin' like? You actin' like a
little fuckin' kid! . . . Silent treatment . . . Thass baby shit!
. . . I had a friend, he usta do the same shit . . . He be mad
at me, he wouldn't say nuthin, juss be silent like a mummy
. . . You a mummy, man? Mofuckin' King Tut? . . . Stupid,
man . . . Tryin' ta punish me? Ain't I punished enough
already? . . . Aaight, fuck you too! I ain't never talkin' to you
again, ever, dass it! . . . Ain't nuttin' interesting 'bout you
anyway! You boring!

Pause.

I'm leavin' here soon anyway. Couple more days, you ain't
never gonna see this face again! Never! Gonna get some
chicken wings and beer! 'Dat shit gonna taste good too! Ice-
cold beer, gonna burn my throat on the way down,
mofuckin' Heineken! Nice flamin' hot wing – gonna dip dat
shit in the bleu cheese, shit gonna be the shit! Gonna go to
the bar: fuckin' Cuba Libre! Gonna get my lawyer drunk,
make love in the bathroom standin' up! Gonna bring juror
number one too, mofuckin' orgy! Gonna leave the
bathroom, tell the waitress: 'Cuba Libre's everywhere!
Libre, mothahfuckah! Whatchu think 'bout dat?!'

Pause.

Whatever I wanna do, I'm a double do dat shit! You like
movies? I ain't talkin' 'bout no Charlton Heston Moses
bullshit, I'm talkin' 'bout mothahfuckin' real movies! I'm a
go to a spot, pick up a big-ass bag a some proper smoke, roll
the most gigantic El you ever fuckin seen, blaze that shit up
till it's ash, and go see every fuckin' movie out there! Tom
Cruise, Al Pacino, Jackie Chan: I'm a see all dat! I'm a get a
popcorn so big, that shit gonna look like a two-story

building! I'm a get a Coca-Cola – that shit gonna be refreshing!

Valdez   Eight minutes!!

Angel   Ain't never gonna hear that voice again neither!

I'm a be Honolulu, Hawaii doin' the dog paddle! I'm a be back ta school, get a degree! I'm a be walkin' down the street, meet my wife – Love at First Sight – buy a carpet and a toaster! I'm a do all a that! . . . You say sumpthin', man? . . . Whatchu said? Even if you ain't said nuttin', I know you thinkin' some shit! Thinkin' some stupid shit . . . Whatchu thinkin'? . . . I know what you thinkin'. C'mon, say it. C'mon mothahfuckah, talk! Yo, whattsamatter, you afraid you ain't got nuthin' ta say? Afraid I'll knock your nonsense right out the fuckin' park? Whatchu gotta say?

Pause.

Fine! Be like that!

Pause.

Lucius   . . . Smell like rain.

Angel   What?

Lucius   I say, it smell like rain.

Valdez   Seven minutes!!

Angel (*to* **Valdez**)   It ain't been no fifty-three minutes, Valdez!

Lucius   He ain't talkin' 'bout how much time you got. He talkin' 'bout how long I got before they escort my ass to the van downstairs.

Angel   You goin ta court?

Lucius   Florida.

Angel   Florida? . . . Today?

Lucius   Why? Was you plannin' ta bake me a cake?

Angel Yo . . . nah, juss, you know . . . I'm juss sayin' . . .

Lucius Sayin' what? 'Sorry'? People don't appreciate no human life! I'm tryin' ta stay alive, make a contribution, everybody outraged: 'How dare he wanna live!' . . . Now, I'm a go die; you think it's gonna make one bit a difference? People still gonna be pissed off: 'Why he got a bed?', 'Why can't we torture him more?', 'Why he eatin a damn cheeseburger?' Fuck 'em.

Angel I'm . . . You can't appeal dat shit?

Lucius I accept God's will.

Angel But, what if dat ain't God's will?

Lucius A lesser man might raise dat question.

Angel I ain't lesser.

Valdez Six minutes!

Lucius Nah, you perfect. You gonna go home, smoke a joint, everything gonna be okey-dokey.

Angel Dass right.

Lucius Wake up in the mornin', eatin' your Fruity Pebbles, talkin' 'bout: 'Gee, Mommy! What a scary dream I had.'

Angel Doan' see why not –

Lucius – 'I didn't really kill no man.' 'I don't really have ta take no responsibilty.' 'God gonna work out a special payment plan for me.'

Angel Yup.

Lucius See I wasn't aware God took the damn Discover card! But I guess if you're 'Angel Cruz', well, it's juss different, huh? Everybody else pay cash, but – 'Angel'? he juss walk right out the store and God'll juss put it on his tab, ain't that right?

Angel You juss jealous I'm gettin out –

Lucius   What I got ta be jealous for? You got Be-elzebub doin' your thinkin' for ya; meanwhile I got the Voice a God sounding sweetly in my ear tellin' me: 'Ya done good, Lucius, now come on home.'

Angel   'Ya done good'?! Lucius, what the fuck 'good' you ever done ta make God say some bullshit like that?

Lucius   Why doan' you ask Him yourself if you're so innerested?

Angel   I'm askin' you.

Lucius   And I'm tellin' you: I ain't no long-distance phone operator! You gotta a question for The Man, you need ta dial direct, jack!

Angel   What's so 'good' 'bout killin' eight people?!

Lucius   'Eight people', 'eight people', dass all anyone ever wanna say!

Angel   Dass cuz –

Lucius   Y'all love ta get all up in Lucius' business, doncha? Makes y'all feel cozy and safe! 'Lucius killed eight people, he bad! We ain't killed no eight people, we must be good!' Shoot, dass some humorous knee-slapper y'all perpetratin' on yourselves – and dass my word right there!

Valdez   Five minutes!

Lucius   Every night, kid, every night, without fail, on the cement ground, knees bruised, ligaments twitchin' an tortin', neck achin', I prayed for you. Asked God: 'Make Angel who he is, not how he actin'' . . . I cried.

Angel   . . . Yeah well –

Lucius   Somethin' wrong wit' 'dat?

Angel   You could do whatchu want –

Lucius   That ain't what I asked ya –

Angel   I'm sayin' –

Lucius   Son: me prayin' for ya, is there somethin' wrong wit dat?

Angel   It ain't wrong –

Lucius   Is it 'bad'?

Angel   I didn't say that –

Lucius   Is it 'bad'?!

Angel   . . . Nah.

Lucius   Is it 'good'?

Angel   Dat don't mean –

Lucius   Don't mean, don't mean! Did it ever occur to you once . . . ever . . . in all these days 'n' nights we spent together: did it ever occur to you, Angel, ever, ever . . . to pray for me?

Pause.

Valdez   Four minutes!!

Pause.

Lucius   . . . See? . . . Dass what I thought . . .

Angel   . . . Lucius –

Lucius   – Doncha 'Lucius' me now! Shoulda 'Lucius'-ed me then!

Angel   God don't hear me.

Lucius   God hear you and you hear God! You doan' like what he sayin', dass the real story!

Angel   I don't know what He's sayin!

Lucius   Get on your knees right now, ask the Lord's forgiveness, I dare ya!

Angel   Yo –

Lucius   Do it!

Angel   And then what?! I get on my knees: 'Forgive me, forgive me, forgive me,' and then what?!

Lucius   You know what!

Angel   Ain't gonna change nuttin'!

Lucius   Coward!!

Angel   I ain't no coward!

Lucius   Then prove it!

Angel   I ain't gots ta prove shit.

Lucius   God say –

Angel   You don't know nuttin' 'bout God –

Lucius   I know everything about God! It's people like you, cryin' in the darkness, waitin' on the lightning, meanwhile you got the flashlight in your own damn lap; you're the ones don't know shit about God! God say: 'Come to Me and Be Free'! How much more Red Carpet rollin' y'all need?! People wait on faith like it's some kinda gift! Ain't nuttin' like that! Faith is like a little blade a grass, fights its way through the concrete tryin' a get hisself a little drink a water! Faith ain't a gift, it's a decision! And I made my decision! I ain't no Puerto Rican Finger Puppet waggin' my head like a fool! I am my own man! I am a soldier of Christ, and the Light a God shines on me and in me in perpetuity, jack!

Angel   You killed eight people –

Lucius   So what I killed eight people? They juss' people!

Angel   . . . What?!

Lucius   If God didn't mean for them people to be killed, how would I have the ability to kill them?!

Angel   Them people never did nothin' wrong.

Lucius   Never said they did.

Angel   You did that shit on your own.

Lucius   Yes I did.

Angel   Not God, you.

Lucius   Dass right.

Angel   Your own Free Will.

Lucius   Hold up now! Was it my Free Will to be molested
and sodomized, abused and violated from the age a five?
Was it my Free Will to turn ta drugs and alcohol as a result
a that shit? Was it my Free Will to be a undiagnosed manic-
depressive paranoid schizophrenic?! Nah, people doan'
wanna hear 'bout none a that! All people wanna do is cry
for the victims! What about my victimization?

Angel   That ain't –

Lucius   They put some faggot-ass Rock Star on VH-1
talkin' 'bout his battle wit' addiction, everybody cry! Some
movie actress, she got incested once or twice, she so 'brave'
to come forward! But me? I'm juss a Black Plague! Ain't no
'disease a addiction' for me, it's 'Free Will'. Ain't no 'brave
comin' forward' for Lucius, it's Florida and death fuckin'
row!

Angel   You crazy, man –

Valdez   3 minutes!

Lucius   Jesus' last words was: 'Forgive them, Father, they
know not what they do.' Now I'm tryin' ta take the Jesus
perspective on this whole deal, forgive the people, but it's
hard. Everybody act like they down wit' God, but didn't
God say killing's wrong?

Angel   Killing's wrong for everyone else, but it's OK for
you?!

Lucius   I killed a little boy, chopped his pee-pee off and
fed it to him. Beat him to death with his own baseball bat,
he was screamin': 'Mommy, Mommy.' It didn't feel wrong.
It felt good!

Angel   That's 'cuz you fucked in the head, man!

Lucius   If that's true, then, what's your excuse?

Angel   I ain't makin' excuses –

Lucius   How'd it feel when you killed that Reverend Kim? Was it good for you too?

Angel   How you gonna enjoy killin' a little kid and think God could ever wanna shine a light on you?!

Valdez   Two minutes!!

Lucius   God loves me.

Angel   He loves you more than He loves an innocent boy?!

Lucius   Do God love you more than He loved dat Reverend Kim?! . . . Huh?! . . . Answer my damn question!

Angel   Maybe He does –

Lucius   – 'Maybe'?! 'Maybe'?! That ain't no answer! Mothahfuckah, get up on that witness stand tomorrow, tell the judge, 'maybe' I shot that Reverend – see what he gonna tell ya! . . . 'Maybe Time' is over, this is 'Grown Man Time' right here! You shot and killed an unarmed, defenseless sixty-five-year-old man. Period. The End. You know it, I know it, God know it! And, you did it in a church! You could dance the lambada 'round it all night, string a forest full a Christmas trees with all the 'maybes' you could pull out your turned-out, lyin' ass – and it will never be different from how I just said it!! . . . Shit! (*To God.*) Try ta offer a dyin' fool in the desert a drink a water, Lord, and all he could say is 'maybe'!!

Angel   I'm goin' home, Lucius – home – and I'm gonna have my life, ya fuckin' lunatic!

Lucius   Bitch, you are home! And the life you have is miserable and worthless and done! And I'm a tell you somethin' else: Proud!, Hateful!, Selfish!, False!, Cowardly!,

Slippery!, Vengeful!, Weak-Willed!, Without Remorse!, Neither Fish nor Fowl: Evil – mothahfuckah – just add water!

Angel 'Just add water'?! . . . Shit, you Betty Crocker, now? Mofuckin' Betty Crocker?! Betty Crock-o-fuckin'-shit! –

Lucius The evil took ya, Angel – took ya so good, you don't even know you gone!

Angel I ain't gone nowhere!

Lucius Oh, you gone, all right. Gone! . . . Bon voyage, Baby Capone – enjoy the chicken wings!

Angel You don't know me! You don't know nuthin'!

Lucius OK.

Angel You don't know my heart! . . . I'm all heart!

Lucius Was.

Angel Shut the fuck up!

Valdez Two minutes!

Angel All your words! All your bullshit! All this time! All this time, I thought you maybe knew sumpthin' –

Lucius I know you killed a man.

Angel Yeah! Yeah, Dass right! Yeah! I killed a man. One man!!

Lucius One's better than eight?

Angel It's different.

Lucius How?

Angel I ain't like you!

Lucius You juss like me!

Angel   I ain't nuthin' like you! I ain't insane, mothahfuckah! I ain't tryin' ta hide behind no religion, and I ain't never did no sicko shit like you!

Lucius   Killin' a man ain't sick?

Angel   I ain't, I can't talk to you no more!

Lucius   You in jail like me, live in a cage like me, took life juss like me! Most people, whether they sick or not, most people don't do no murder like we done – yeah, dass right mothahfuckah, I said 'we'! So how the fuck you so different from me?!

Angel   I know who I am!

Lucius   Don't know shit!

Angel   I know who I am! I'm good!

Lucius   You ain't good!

Angel   Mothahfuckah, I don't feed little children their dicks, then say it felt good! I don't say shooting the Reverend Kim felt good! I know what I did! I know how I feel –

Lucius   I 'know' how the Reverend Kim 'feels' – mothahfuckah feels dead!!

Angel   I'm goin' home!!

Lucius   You ain't nuthin' but a pigeon-hearted little bitch – thass your nature, thass your character, thass who you are!

Angel   You don't know me!

Lucius   Yeah, you might be lookin' at me, but you talkin' 'bout your own self, ain'tcha?!

Angel   I ain't, I won't, wouldn't . . .

Lucius   'Won't wouldn't' what?! What?!

Angel (*to* **Valdez**)   Valdez!

Lucius   Valdez can't save ya!

Angel (*to* **Valdez**)   Valdez, Take me outta here!

Lucius   You ain't no man! You ain't shit, you don't stand for shit, and your life is a wasteful embarrassment!

Angel   Valdez!!

Lucius   Oldest juvenile delinquent I ever seen! Still squirt dog-water, doncha?

Angel   Fuck you.

Lucius   Got no vocabulary neither! Unrepentant no class sinner!

Angel   Yo, Valdez!!

Lucius   Run back ta the darkness, ya blind bat!

Angel   I ain't nuthin' like you!

Lucius   Proud, proud, proud!

Angel   Never was, never will be!

Lucius   Chirp, chirp, chirp!

Angel   Valdez!

Valdez   One minute!

Angel   C'mon, Valdez!

Valdez   One minute!

Angel   Valdez!! Please!!

Valdez   One minute!!

Blackout.

Scene Five

Mary Jane   When I used to be a lawyer, I would wake up cranky as hell every morning at 5 a.m. and I would fantasize about sleeping in, of calling in sick, of having a 'me' day. I

was resentful about the demands of the job, the lack of
recognition, the lack of a life . . . the fact that it was 'hard'
. . . Once I got disbarred, . . . I suddenly had all the time in
the world, and I didn't want it . . . I didn't want it at all . . .
Angel's redirect had been masterfully constructed, and he
was masterful. He was wiping away tears, looking the jury
right in the eye, and most of all, he looked and sounded
completely sympathetic and believable . . . I got emotional. I
tried not to show it, but it just spilled out . . . I was proud of
him. I was prouder of myself . . . And why not? . . . It was
my defining moment and . . . I held on to it a split second
too long. Angel started sobbing, and I was vaguely thinking:
'OK, get him off the stand,' but before I could react,
because the truth is I really was getting off on how
emotionally involved the jury was getting over all this,
before I knew what was happening, Angel started talking.
He told the judge not to blame me, that I was just trying to
help. I tried to cut him off, I said: 'No more questions,' but
Angel kept on talking . . .

Angel   'Hail Mary –

Mary Jane   And talking . . .

Angel   'Hail Mary –

Mary Jane   Angel will be eligible for parole in 2028 . . .

Angel   . . . 'Hail Mary, you're a lady, talk to your fuckin'
son' . . . I doan', I doan' mean that . . . I juss, . . . I juss
wanna be good . . . I wanna be, I wanna be a good man,
Mary, I wanna be a man . . . Saint Anthony?! . . . Saint
Anthony!: 'Saint Anthony, Saint Anthony, please come
around, somethin' is lost and – . . . I juss, . . . it's 'cuz . . . I
stole John Hameric's jacket, God. I know you know that,
but I stole it and I'm sorry, and I didn't mean it, even
though I did mean it 'cuz I was jealous that he had that
jacket and I didn't and he cried and cried and I threw that
shit in the Hudson and I never toal' him 'cuz I blamed
Sidney Betincourt and then Sidney Betincourt kicked John's
ass and I never said shit and I am so fuckin' sorry! . . . I am

so fuckin' sorry, God, and please, do somethin' good for
John Hameric wherever he is, make somethin' good happen
to him, please, let him hit the number or find some money
or get a new jacket, God, somethin'! Make him have a good
life 'cuz he loved that fuckin' jacket, God, that fuckin' stupid
Spiderman jacket . . . I can't believe – I wish – I'm so sorry.
I am. Tell his mother, God, 'cuz I know she's with you,
please tell Miss Hameric I'm sorry 'cuz I am sorry; and –

Valdez *enters.*

Valdez   Cruz!

Angel   I am so sorry, I am so, so sorry –

Valdez   Let's go, Cruz.

Angel   I am a man, God! I am a man that is sorry.

Valdez   Cruz! . . .

Angel   I am a man and I am so, so sorry.

Valdez   Cruz! Time!

Angel   Really, God, I'm . . . I . . . Valdez . . . Valdez, I'm
sorry –

Valdez   Step away from the cage.

Angel   I'm, I'm sorry, ya know, Valdez. Valdez: I'm sorry.

Valdez   Quite all right.

Angel   I –

Valdez   Yes . . . Yes . . . Away from the cage

Angel *assumes the position.* **Valdez** *enters, cuffs* **Angel** *and leads
him out of his cage.*